the origins of modern town planning

the origins of modern town planning

by *Leonardo Benevolo*
translated by *Judith Landry*

THE M.I.T. PRESS
Massachusetts Institute of Technology, Cambridge, Massachusetts

Translated from the Italian
LE ORIGINI DELL'URBANISTICA MODERNA
(*Editori Laterza, Bari, 1963*)
English translation
© Routledge & Kegan Paul Ltd. 1967

Library of Congress Catalog Card Number 67—17494
Printed in Great Britain

contents

The republic of the equal, that great hospice open to all men
From the *Manifesto of the Equals*, 1796

illustrations in the text

plates

preface

The birth of modern town-planning did not coincide with the technical and economic movements which created and transformed the industrial town; it emerged later, when these changes began to be felt to their full extent and when they began to conflict, making some kind of corrective intervention inevitable.

Even today town-planning technique invariably lags behind the events it is supposedly controlling, and it retains a strictly remedial character. It is therefore important to examine the first attempts at town-planning that were applied to an industrial society in order to discover the reasons for the original time-lag.

The aim of this book is, primarily, to emphasize the two-fold origin, technical and ideological, of these experiments, and to provide a reconstruction of the two factors which inspired the first reformers: the economic and social changes which produced the inequalities of the first decades of the nineteenth century, and the changes in political theory and public opinion which meant that these disparities were no longer accepted as inevitable but were regarded as obstacles that could and should be removed.

The first attempts to right the evils of the industrial town found expression in two antithetical schools of thought. One adhered to the view that planning must start again from scratch (and in this case new and purely theoretical types of community were planned, quite distinct from the existing towns); the other that each problem must be dealt with, and each defect remedied, separately, without taking into account their inter-relationship and without having any over-all vision of the town as a single organism.

The so-called Utopians—Owen, St.-Simon, Fourier, Cabet, Godin—belonged to the first group, though they did not merely write about their ideal cities, like More, Campanella or Bacon, but agitated for their realization in practical terms. The second group included the specialists and officials who introduced the new health regulations and services into the towns and who, because they had to find the technical and legalistic means to implement these improvements, laid the real foundations of modern town-planning legislation.

Most of these achievements, even the most purely technical, had their roots firmly planted in matters of ideology, which in turn corresponded largely with the beginnings of modern socialism, so much so that the history of these early stages is to be sought in works on the history of economics and socialism, rather than in specialized technical studies.

But this connection lasted only until 1848, the moment when the working-class movement began to be organized in opposition to the parties of the *bourgeoisie*; indeed, planning experiments of the time were influenced by a wide range of ideological trends, from the egalitarian communism of Cabet to French neo-Catholicism.

The working-class movement reached its decisive turning-point with the advent of Marx and Engels, and Marxist Socialism, intent on explaining the 1848 Revolution and its failure in strictly political terms, stressed the contradictions of the earlier movements but completely lost sight of the link between tendencies in politics and in town-planning which, even if formulated in over-simplified terms, had previously been firmly maintained.

From that time onwards political theory almost always tended to disparage specialist research and experiment, and attempted to assimilate proposals for partial reform within the reform of society generally. Town-planning, on the other hand, cut adrift from political discussion, tended to become increasingly a purely technical matter at the service of the established powers. This did not mean, however, that it became politically neutral; on the contrary, it fell within the sphere of influence of the new conservative ideology which was evolving during these years, of Bonapartism in France, of the reforming Tory groups in England and of Bismarckian imperialism in Germany.

This was the explanation for the uncommitted and dependent nature of the main experiments in town-planning after 1848, behind which loomed the political paternalism of the new right.

This is the book's main thesis which is not without relevance to present-day problems. For progressive tendencies of modern planning can be practically realized only if they make contact once more with those political forces which tend towards a similar general transformation of society.

The last thirty years have taught people to recognize the essentially political nature of all decisions taken in town-planning, but this recognition remains purely theoretical as long as town-planning is thought of as an isolated set of interests which must then be brought into contact with politics—a view which grew directly out of the gulf which opened up between the two in 1848.

Although their ideas of planning were somewhat rudimentary, Owen and Chadwick did demonstrate the simple truth that town-planning, though it is a part of politics, and thus necessary to the realization of any effective programme, cannot be identified simply with planning in general.

To achieve a more satisfactory distribution of human activity throughout the country, there must be an improvement in the economic and social relationships on which such activities depend;

on the other hand, improved economic and social relationships do not automatically bring with them a satisfactory utilization of space—on the contrary, a planned use of space is rather one method, inseparable from any other, of creating the over-all balance which is the aim of all political action.

The phases and methods of this action are infinitely more complex than Owen supposed, but the objective of his Utopia is still valid for town-planning today: 'to come to an arrangement which is advantageous to everyone, within a system which will permit continued and unlimited technical improvement.'

I have already attempted to trace these events briefly in the *Storia dell'architttura Moderna* published three years ago by Laterza. I have been drawn back to the same subject not by dialectical necessity, which might possibly be premature, but by several recent developments which have revealed the urgent need for the definition of a new relationship between town-planning and politics, hence between town-planning and social and economic planning. I now believe that I have identified the weak point in my earlier work, i.e. the failure to correlate developments in the fields of architecture and town-planning, to the basic changes in the political scene between 1830 and 1850, and particularly to the crisis of 1848. The present work will also, I hope, correct the earlier account of the events of the turn of the century, and make for a better understanding of the *avant-guarde* movements from Morris onwards. In fact the whole of the *Storia dell'Archittura moderna* could be revised in this way without contradicting the spirit in which it was written, since it is obvious that the accuracy of a historical work which takes into account the practical affairs of the present, is by nature short-lived; this merely indicates that the assumptions upon which such a work is based are continually changing, and that the recent past must be constantly reassessed.

the growth of
the industrial town

The history of modern town-planning was initially a history of
bare facts: it was only later that the changes wrought in the towns
and countryside by the Industrial Revolution emerged and began
to be recognized as real problems, by which time they were already
fairly extensive.

The first decisive change was the increase in population brought
about by the fall in the death-rate which was notably below the
birth-rate for the first time.[1] This increase also produced a change
within the pattern of the population itself: it increased the per-
centage of young people because of the fall in infant mortality and,
most important of all, it upset the age-old balance of nature,
whereby each generation had tended to replace the preceding one

[1] From 1760 onwards England's population began to increase rapidly. Modern
calculations, based on burial and baptism figures, show that in 1700 the population
of England and Wales was 5½ million, and 6½ million in 1750; but in 1801, when
the first census was taken, it had already risen to 9 million, and to 14 million in 1831.
It is also known that the birth-rate—after a slight increase during the first four
decades of the eighteenth century—remained more or less constant throughout the
period, varying from 36·6 to 37·7 per thousand, while immigration from other
countries does not seem to have been very great and was certainly less intense than
emigration to the colonies. On the other hand mortality, temporarily high until

and then to suffer the same fate. All subsequent generations found themselves in a completely new situation and had to find new means of solving an unprecedented problem.

As the population grew, the economic changes that were taking place altered its distribution throughout the country. The most important of the changes concerned the organization of labour and laid the foundations for a complete change in methods of production, which in turn had further repercussions on organization, hastening the development and concentration of the new economic system. For this reason the changing patterns of settlement, motivated by initial organizational changes and intensified by technical innovations, assumed the proportions of a real crisis, shattering the old balance between town and country and creating new tensions, the solution of which was definitely a long-term affair.

It is important now to take a closer look at the effects of the economic changes on urban and rural communities which took place between 1760 and 1830.

The disappearance of the 'open field' system around the old English villages meant that the land could be better utilized, but it also gradually transformed the smaller yeomen into mere tenants or labourers, bound to a set standard of living little above the minimum necessary for survival.[2] The alternative to this was industrial work, particularly in the weaving industry which had long been organized in the country, in the workers' own homes.

[2] In 1795 the obligatory subsidy that the parish paid to needy labourers was regulated by the Speenhamland resolution, which laid down that every family had the right

---

1740 because of famines and alcoholism, fell gradually from 35·8 per thousand during the decade 1730–40 to 21·1 per thousand during 1811–21. Among the causes mentioned by Ashton for this decline in the mortality rate were the introduction of root crops, which made cattle-rearing easier in winter and made a supply of fresh meat possible all the year round; the substitution of wheat for other cereals and an increase in the consumption of vegetables, a higher standard of personal cleanliness, associated with more soap and cheaper cotton underwear; the use of brick in place of timber for walls and of slate and stone in place of thatch for roofs; a decrease in the number of industrial occupations carried out in the workers' own dwellings; progress in medicine and surgery, and more hospitals and dispensaries; a more rational placing of refuse dumps and cemeteries; and better drainage and water supplies in the towns. (cf. T. S. Ashton, *The Industrial Revolution*, London, 1947.)

But the old family organization, whereby the processes of spinning, weaving and dyeing were carried out by the same family, who also bought the raw wool and sold the finished product, was too static and unproductive to keep pace with the demands of an ever-expanding market. Traders preferred to provide the raw material and take back the finished product, paying their workers on a piece-work basis and entrusting groups of specialized workers with the various processes.

But once the greater productivity margins of this system too were in turn exhausted, competition demanded a further decrease in costs and increase in quantity, and stimulated a series of technical inventions which radically altered working conditions.

The weavers were using the machine invented in 1733 by the watchmaker J. Kay (the 'fly shuttle') which enabled each weaver to work alone at the loom without a helper to lay the threads; but because of the impossibility of producing spun yarn in sufficient quantities, production was still limited until the year 1764, when the carpenter Hargreaves invented a new type of spinning machine (the 'jenny') which enabled a single worker to manage several threads at once.

The jenny and fly shuttle began to be used in country dwellings in the wool and cotton districts, revolutionizing the existence of every able-bodied member of the family. But the quantity of yarn and cloth produced by each machine was necessarily limited by the energy that could be exerted by physical labour; to produce more,

to a minimum wage, regulated by the price of bread, and that the parish was to supplement the actual wages earned by a man in order to bring them up to that level: 'when the gallon loaf of second flour, weighing eight pounds eleven ounces, shall cost one shilling, then every poor and industrious man shall have for his own support three shillings weekly, either produced by his own or his family's labour or an allowance from the poor rates, and for the support of his wife and every other member of the family, one shilling and sixpence. When the gallon loaf shall cost one and fourpence, then every poor and industrious man shall have four shillings weekly for his own, and one and tenpence for the support of every other member of his family. And so in proportion . . .' (From J. L. and B. Hammond, *The Village Labourer*, London, 1919, p. 163.)

In this way the poor rate helped to keep agricultural wages low—until 1834, when the system was abolished—by ensuring labourers the minimum necessary for subsistence but excluding any possible improvement in their condition.

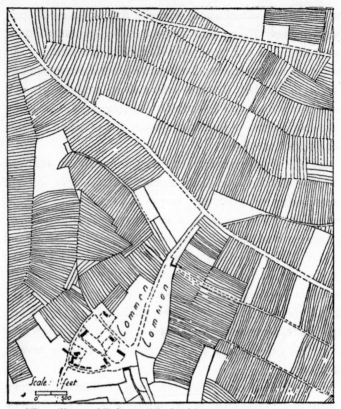

1 The village of Balscott (Oxfordshire) in 1768, with the common land farmed in small strips (from T. Sharp, *English Panorama*).

manpower would have to be replaced by some mechanical force.

In 1771 a barber from Preston, R. Arkwright, invented the first spinning machine worked by water (the 'water frame') and in 1775 the weaver S. Crompton began to experiment with a more highly-developed machine, based on a cross between the jenny and the new water frame.

These inventions gave spinning a temporary advantage over weaving, which lasted until 1784 when the Reverend E. Cartwright invented the first mechanical loom; soon afterwards, between 1785 and 1790, water power was replaced by Watt's steam engine, patented in 1769.

4

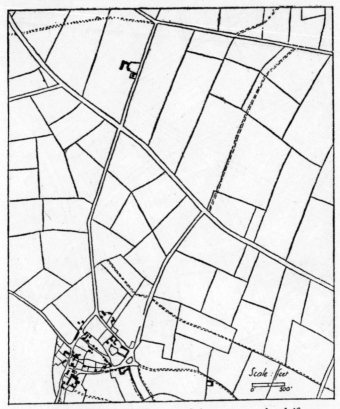

2   The same village, after the enclosure of the common land (from Sharp).

This forced the weaving industry to abandon its former scattered organization and to concentrate in large workshops where the necessary energy was available, at first near water courses and, later, near coal-mines, as coal was needed to fuel Watt's steam engine. The steam-engine in its turn solved the problem of the seepage of water in the mines, revolutionizing the techniques of extraction and transforming the mine itself into a modern workshop.

The same period saw Darby's coke substituted ever more widely for charcoal in the smelting of iron ore, and in 1783 H. Cort discovered how to utilize coal in forging and rolling. This put the

5

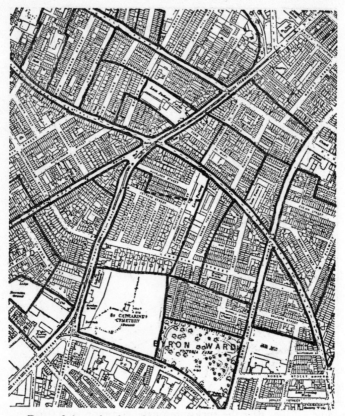

3 Part of the suburbs of Nottingham, where building followed the line of the enclosures (from W. C. Hoskins, *The Making of English Landscape*).

iron industry in a position to supply the new mechanized industry, and foundries, like blast-furnaces, moved from wooded regions to those with coal, with the result that large self-contained plants tended to grow up.

Thus in the space of a single generation, between 1760 and 1790, a degree of technical progress was achieved which made unlimited increase in industrial production possible.[3] The development of

[3] Iron production rose from 17,000 tons in 1740 to 650,000 in 1830; in 1764 (when the Jenny was invented) the cotton industry worked 3,800,000 pounds a year, increasing in 1775—with the appearance of the steam loom—to 18 million, to 123 million in 1810 and 273 million in 1830.

these industries and their concentration in large factories drew many families from the agricultural districts of the south to the mining districts of the midlands and north, from isolated country dwellings to the cramped districts that were built near the factories[4]; so new towns were born, while old ones grew out of all proportion.

The connection between towns and industry was soon very close. In the new towns, which had grown up outside the system of boroughs and parishes, contractors and workmen could escape the anachronistic bonds of the Elizabethan guild system; contractors could draw on an ever-plentiful and easily replaceable reserve of labour; the workmen themselves, although mercilessly exploited by their new masters, now had a wider range of choice as well as the possibility of gaining recognition as a body[5] and of organizing themselves in order to protect their common interests.

Meanwhile the demands of trade, and in particular the need for transport for heavy goods such as coal and iron ore, resulted in an overhaul of the networks of communication. The rough parish roads were replaced, after 1745, by new turnpikes built by private companies, after 1760 estuaries and navigable rivers were linked by new canals and other private companies organized boat and stage-coach services on canals and roads, to carry both passengers and goods. In 1767 R. Reynolds built the first cast-iron railway-line for carrying coal, and 1801 saw the inauguration of the Surrey Iron Railway, the first enterprise of its kind for carrying goods. It was only after 1825, however, with the invention of Stephenson's locomotive, that the railways, which were to have so decisive an influence during the following decade, really began to develop.

[4] Manchester was a village of 12,000 inhabitants in the middle of the eighteenth century but by 1800 it was a town of 95,000 and by 1850 of 400,000. Between the middle of the eighteenth and the middle of the nineteenth century Glasgow grew from a city of 30,000 to one of 300,000 inhabitants and Leeds grew from 17,000 to 170,000. In France Mulhouse had 10,000 inhabitants in 1812 and 36,000 in 1836, Roubaix had 8,000 in 1816 and 65,000 in 1866. (cf. Lavedan, *Histoire de l'urbanisme*, Vol. III, Paris, 1958.)

[5] The first workers' associations, which had grown up in opposition to the traditional guilds, were forbidden by French law in 1791 and by English law in 1800; the laws were repealed in 1813 and 1824 respectively.

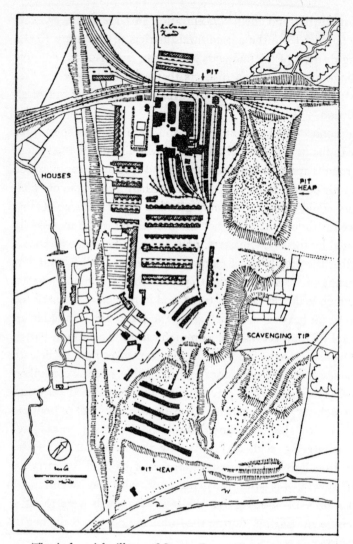

4 The industrial village of Sunny Brow, Durham (from Sharp).

It is in relation to this new transport system and to the ever-expanding commercial activity that the unprecedented growth of certain towns must be viewed; it was in these towns that the main trade routes converged and they were the financial and admini-

8

5 Network of English rivers and canals in 1800 (from E. L. Bogart, *Economic History of Europe*).

strative pivots of the new economy. London, which already had a million inhabitants at the end of the eighteenth century, had 2,235,000 in 1841, making it the largest city that was or ever had been.

9

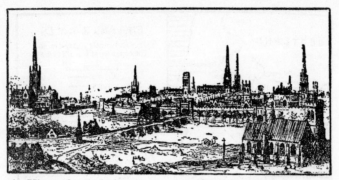

6 View of a Catholic city in 1440 (from A. W. Pugin, *Contrasts*, 1836).

Collectively, these changes caused the majority of England's population to alter both their place of residence and their way of life, revolutionized the use of land and modified the appearance of the countryside. The extent of these phenomena—the increase in town-dwellers, the productive capacity of the new industrial and commercial establishments, the miles of new roads and canals and the number of vehicles circulating on town roads—was unprecedented, and so was the speed with which they took place. Towns were born and doubled their size within a generation, projects for factories, roads and canals were carried out with startling swiftness, mines were opened up in the heart of hitherto virgin agricultural countryside, blast-furnaces and factory chimneys rose to the sky side by side with cathedral spires.

The political and economic thought of the time was affected less by the building up of new structures than by the decline of traditional ones, and the majority of its theories were concerned with opposition to the restrictions and institutions hindering the free expansion of the new enterprises.

Political reformers used rational criticism to demolish the privileges of absolutism, social hierarchy and economic planning and, though they devoted much thought to safeguarding the citizen against the abuses of authority, they were extremely vague about the way the new State was to be organized. This was con-

10

7   View of the same Catholic city in 1840 (from Pugin).

ceived ideally as an empty space within which the individual and
the public came into direct contact with one another without any
mediating structure to trouble their relationship: the realization
of the democratic ideal was apparently tailored to include the
absorption of all the 'partial associations' within the sovereign
'republic'.[6]

Such theories, while stressing political and constitutional problems in general, did tend to belittle the organizational problems
of the various sectors, or to reduce them to mere deductions to be
made from these general theories.

Each difficulty met with, in connection with the survival of a
traditional institution, encouraged the formation of theories
which excluded any form of public intervention in that sector.
During the famine of 1797 Malthus put forward his population
theory, which demonstrated the uselessness of all laws for the
relief of the poor, and in 1817, during the post-war depression,
Ricardo published his treatise on political economy advocating
the abolition of Customs and Excise.

Thus while liberal thought was successfully brushing aside the
old restrictions of laws and customs—a revolution which, in
Europe and America, was almost completed between 1776 and

[6] This is the terminology used by Rousseau in his *Contrat social* of 1762; cf. *The
Social Contract,* tr. H. J. Tozer, London, 1905, Ch. III, 'Whether the General Will
Can Err'.

1832—the towns and countryside were left practically without any adequate measures for town and country planning.

The most advanced section of economic and political thought persuaded both governments and public opinion against interference, blinded them to the problems that were arising from the changes in the use of land and discredited and weakened the traditional methods of town-planning, though it did not suggest any new ones to replace them and merely outlined suggestions for an absurd extension of *laissez faire*. Adam Smith, for example, advised governments to sell their State property in order to settle their debts.

Examples of Baroque town-planning and particularly certain illustrious buildings of the first half of the eighteenth century, are often impressive anticipations of the spatial dimension of the modern town (one can imagine the avenues of Versailles transformed into the 'boulevards' of a late nineteenth-century town, just as the radiating avenues of the Champs Elysées became the basis for Haussmann's Etoile) whereas the time factor, which was to be so important in the new urban society, remained totally foreign to them.

Previously the face of a town had altered so slowly that, at any given moment, it could be regarded as static for an indefinite period of time. To lay out a square, a district or a whole town was to give it a definitive and permanent architectural form, though sufficient margin was allowed to absorb, without basic alteration, any foreseeable future growth; in other words, it was to apply the plausible approximation of an absolutely invariable image to a very slow-moving reality.

But this approximation became increasingly difficulty as the tempo of change became more and more rapid, and at the same time liberal thought was destroying belief in the intervention of authority upon which the effective execution of this type of operation depended. For this reason, from the second half of the eighteenth century—when in the sphere of planning monumental complexes and setting them tastefully amid the surrounding

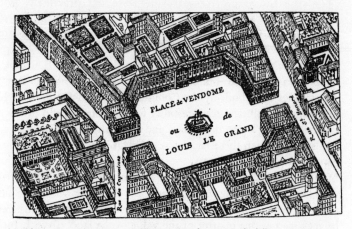

8   Paris, Place Vendôme (from Turgot's plan, 1734). The square was
designed by Mansart between 1685 and 1699, in honour of Louis
XIV, but from 1677 onwards the architect had joined with other
financiers to acquire and divide up the surrounding sites. When these
sites were offered up for sale, it was decreed that 'the purchasers of
the sites facing on to the square will become the owners of the
façades which His Majesty caused to be built, and they will be able
to purchase the length they require, provided that it is not less than
two spans. The purchasers of the land around the square and the
neighbouring streets will not be required to pay any dues, apart from
the compensation payable to the original owners, as stated in the
decree of the Council of State of 2 May 1686.'

townscape or countryside architecture had reached its finest
expression—there was a decline in executive coherence and in the
ability of any ruling body to cut deep into the fabric of the towns.

The architectural regularity of the royal squares of Paris was
achieved by imposing a uniform façade on many independent
houses. But Louis XIII played a decisive part in the creation of
the Place des Vosges (completed in 1609) by reserving ownership
of the axial 'pavillions'; Mansart (1685–99) designed the façades
only of Place Vendôme and Place des Victoires for Louis XIV,
which were then sold to the owners of the sites, and he also contributed to several of the other building projects which were
carried out in fairly rapid succession. In the same way, in the

13

Place de la Concorde, Gabriel built the façades of the two build-ings at the head of, and flanking, the Rue Royale (1755–63) for Louis XV, but the actual buildings behind these façades were completed many years later, and in the Rue de Rivoli in 1805 the architects of Napoleon I, Percier and Fontaine, designed only the architectural part of the façades, whose acceptance and construc-tion was binding upon the purchasers.

Similarly, many of the most admired complexes of the late eighteenth century in England—the Circus and Royal Crescent in Bath (J. Wood, 1764 and 1769), the famous squares of Blooms-bury (1775–1827) and, later, Regent's Park (J. Nash, 1812)— consisted in the superimposition of a uniform architecture upon a number of separate houses; symmetry and unity of perspective, originally the elements of structural planning, had now become the vehicle for mere external uniformity. The sophistication and elegance of these last products of the classical tradition concealed its estrangement, now complete, from the problems of the new town and precluded any contact between this tradition and the situation which was growing out of the Industrial Revolution.

While the rich middle classes continued to gather in the exquisite settings of such places as Bedford Place and Russell

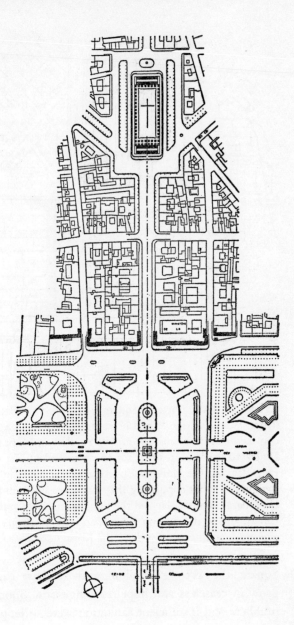

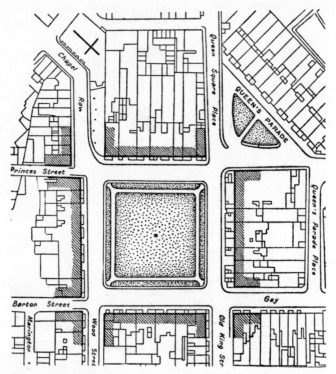

10 ABOVE Bath, Queen's Square 11 OPPOSITE Bath Royal Crescent
(from Auzelle). John Wood began his career as an architect and
contractor in Bath with the architectural complex of Queen's Square.
He leased the land in 1724, for 99 years, and sub-let the sites for 98
years, leaving the individual purchasers free to design the interiors of
the buildings but stipulating that they have uniform façades masking
the separate houses. He did the same thing, later, with the Royal
Circus, and so did his son John Wood the Younger, on a more
ambitious architectural scale in the Royal Crescent (1769).

Square, the wretched buildings in the East End continued to
grow in ceaseless and hopeless congestion. Soon overwhelming
numbers and insufficient sanitation were to jeopardize the well-
being of the whole city, and a completely new methodology,
without any points of contact with the old, had to be evolved to
deal with the problem.

16

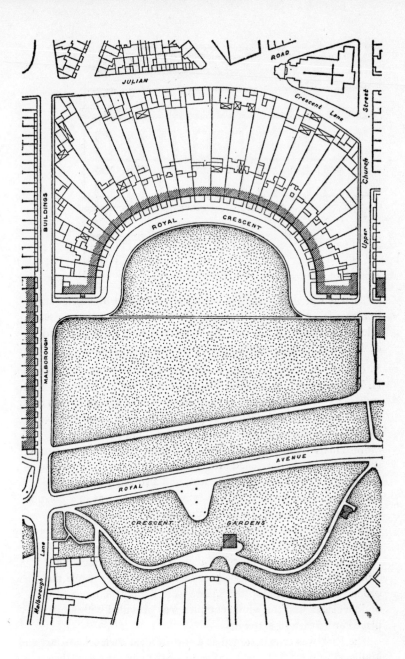

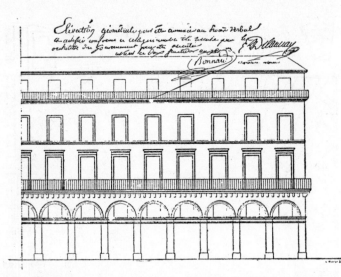

12 Paris, Rue de Rivoli. The façade was designed by Percier and Fontaine in 1806 and was imposed on all the buildings on the north side of the street. In this case the Municipal authorities provided the design only, leaving construction to private individuals.

13 OPPOSITE London, John Nash's plans for the Prince Regent (from H. R. Hitchcock, *Architecture, Nineteenth and Twentieth centuries*). Nash embarked on the project in 1812, to make use of a large stretch of Crown land; the public Park—Regent's Park—was created between 1820–30, together with the houses that surround it, and the new thoroughfare from Piccadilly Circus—Regent's Street—was opened through a densely populated area. Nash built some of the buildings around the park and along the street, and also acted as a private contractor, when in 1813, as Surveyor General, he was in a position to co-ordinate the enterprises of other planners and contractors.

In his design for Regent's Park, Nash collaborated with Humphrey Repton. It included several isolated villas and two groups of cottages, some classical in style, others Tudor; the terraces built around the Park were designed for the rich *bourgeoisie,* while the groups of houses in Munster Square were within the range of the middle classes and the whole complex was provided with a market placed at its eastern extremity.

The Park was thus designed as a sort of ideal enclave, abstract and idyllic, cut off from the real problems of the city that were then multiplying so rapidly, as Chadwick was trying to demonstrate.

18

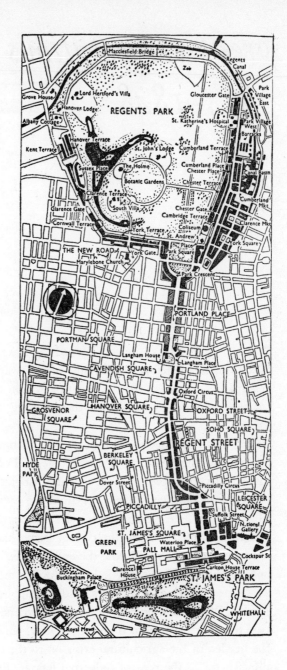

C

great expectations
1815-1848

When, in June 1815, England learned the news of the victory of Waterloo, the relief at the ending of the war was soon overshadowed by concern for the situation within the country itself, for there were many problems that military success could not solve.

The old king, George III, was mad and his duties were performed by the dissolute Prince Regent. Foreign policy was directed by the cold and unpopular Castlereagh, who was to commit suicide seven years later amid the indifference and hostility of his fellow-countrymen. War expenses had produced progressive inflation, and the cost of living had almost doubled between 1790 and 1813; now the ending of war restrictions was endangering the monopoly held by English merchants on ocean routes and by English farmers in their supplies to the national market. Parliament, dominated by land-owners, was preparing to pass the disastrous protectionist Corn Law, which was to transfer the burden of the agricultural crisis on to the consumer and, indirectly, on to the cost of industrial labour. Fear of the French

Revolution had transformed many enlightened conservatives, such as Burke, into advocates of violence, and had encouraged the government to repress any signs of non-conformism with unusual severity.

Meanwhile the Industrial Revolution and the rise in population had already radically transformed the distribution of the populace throughout the country and, in the absence of suitable measures of control, the inadequacies of the new centres began to make themselves felt.

The families who were moving out of the countryside and into these industrial centres were housed either in empty accommodation available in the older quarters, or in new buildings on the outskirts, which soon multiplied to form new and extensive districts around the original nuclei.

The building of the new houses or the conversion of existing ones was carried out by private speculators—the 'jerry builders'—and the element of competition meant that the quality of the houses, as well as the wages and working hours of the men who built them, were, almost everywhere, the worst that working-class families would put up with. Rents varied very little, being closely linked with wages, which were themselves the minimum compatible with the survival of the worker; the profits on the original capital could therefore be increased only by reducing the outlay and building houses of the lowest possible quality. Furthermore most of the working-class dwellings of Manchester, Birmingham, Leeds and the London suburbs were built during the Napoleonic wars, when timber imported from the Baltic countries was already becoming scarce, labour more expensive and, above all, when interest rates on capital were already increasing, and were to remain high long after the end of the war. Wartime conditions, in fact, had a decisive effect on the poor quality of the new districts.

Despite all this, the houses occupied by working-class families in the towns were probably no worse, taken individually, than the country dwellings they had originally inhabited.

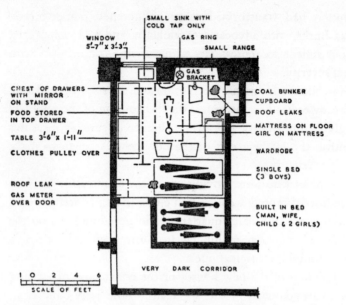

The figure contains the following labels:

SMALL SINK WITH COLD TAP ONLY

GAS RING

SMALL RANGE

WINDOW 5'-7" x 3'-3"

GAS BRACKET

CHEST OF DRAWERS WITH MIRROR ON STAND

FOOD STORED IN TOP DRAWER

TABLE 3'-6" x 1'-11"

CLOTHES PULLEY OVER

ROOF LEAK

GAS METER OVER DOOR

COAL BUNKER

CUPBOARD

ROOF LEAKS

MATTRESS ON FLOOR
GIRL ON MATTRESS

WARDROBE

SINGLE BED
(3 BOYS)

BUILT IN BED
(MAN, WIFE, CHILD & 2 GIRLS)

VERY DARK CORRIDOR

1 O   2   4   6
SCALE OF FEET

14   Glasgow, an overcrowded dwelling still in existence in 1948
(from *Journal of the Royal Institute of British Architects,* 1948).

The walls were of brick rather than of timber, the roofs were of
slate or stone rather than thatch, the rooms were smaller, but not
cluttered with the bulk and dirt of family spinning-machines and
sanitation was lacking or equally primitive in both cases.

The differences are more striking, on the other hand, if one
considers:

(*a*) the problems connected with the relationship between houses
and other buildings, within the limited confines of the industrial
town;

(*b*) the inhabitants' change of attitude towards the hardships
which they were forced to suffer.

Inadequate sanitation, relatively bearable in the country, became
impossible in the town because of the overcrowding of the vast
number of new buildings.

As long as each house was detached, refuse, liquid and solid,
could easily be disposed of and the various outdoor activities—

the rearing of animals, the children's games, the movement of carts and pedestrians—could be carried on without much mutual annoyance. But now the density and sheer size of the new working-class districts made refuse disposal almost impossible: open sewers ran along beside the roads, every available corner was piled high with rubbish. Carts and pedestrians, animals and playing children jostled one another in the fight for space.

Residential quarters naturally tended to be built near the place of work, so that houses and factories were often in close contact, intermingled at random and mutually inconvenient. Factory smoke permeated the houses and factory waste polluted the water, while industrial movement was generally hopelessly impeded by private traffic.

This chaos was constantly aggravated by the dynamic nature of the factors involved: factories were transformed and expanded, houses were demolished and rebuilt, the outskirts of the cities crept further into the countryside without ever finding a definitive balance.

The following is the classic description of Manchester written by Engels in 1845, making use of data provided by the research and studies of the previous decades:

(In the old town) the streets, even the better ones, are narrow and winding ... the houses dirty, old and tumble-down, and the construction of the side streets utterly horrible. Going from the old church to Long Millgate, the stroller has at once a row of old-fashioned houses at the right, of which not one has kept its original level; these are the remnants of the old pre-manufacturing Manchester, whose former inhabitants have removed with their descendants into better-built districts and have left the houses, which were not good enough for them, to a population strongly mixed with Irish blood. Here one is in an almost undisguised working-man's quarter, for even the shops and beer-houses hardly take the trouble to exhibit a trifling degree of cleanliness. But all this is nothing in comparison with the courts and lanes which lie behind, to which access can be gained only through covered passages, in which no two human beings can pass at the same time. Of the irregular cramming together of dwellings which defy all

23

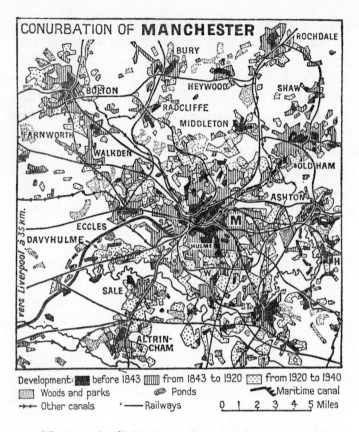

15   The growth of Manchester (from P. George, *Les Villes*).

rational plan, of the tangle in which they are crowded literally one upon the other, it is impossible to convey an idea. And it is not the buildings surviving from the old times of Manchester which are to blame for this; the confusion has only recently reached its height when every scrap of space left by the old way of building has been filled up and patched over until not a foot of land is left to be further occupied.

This sketch should be sufficient to show the absurd planning of the whole district, particularly along the Irk. The south bank of this river is here very steep and between fifteen and thirty feet high. On this declivitous hillside there are planted three rows of houses, of which the lowest rise directly out of the river, while the front walls of the

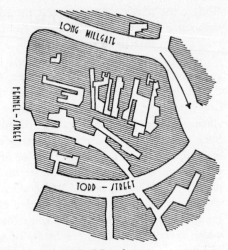

16   Sketch of the district bordering the Irk, Manchester.

highest stand on the crest of the hill in Long Millgate. Among them
are mills on the river, in short, the method of construction is as crowded
and disorderly here as in the lower part of Long Millgate. Right and
left a multitude of covered passages lead from the main street into
numerous courts, and he who turns in thither gets into a filth and
disgusting grime the equal of which is not to be found—especially in
the courts which lead down to the Irk, and which contain unqualifiedly
the most horrible dwellings I have yet beheld. In one of these courts
there stands directly at the entrance a privy without a door, so dirty
that the inhabitants can pass into and out of that court only by passing
through foul pools of urine and excrement. This is the first court of
the Irk above Ducie Bridge—in case anyone should care to look at it.
Below it on the river there are several tanneries which fill the whole
neighbourhood with the stench of animal putrefaction. Below Ducie
Bridge the only entrance to most of the houses is by means of narrow,
dirty stairs and over heaps of refuse and filth. The first court below
Ducie Bridge, known as Allen's Court, was in such a state at the time
of the cholera that the sanitary police ordered it evacuated, swept and
disinfected with chloride of lime. Dr. Kay gives a terrible description
of the state of this court at that time.[1] Since then, it seems to have
been partially torn away and rebuilt; at least looking down from Ducie

[1] J. P. Kay, *The Moral and Physical Condition of the Working Classes, Employed in the
Cotton Manufacture in Manchester,* London, 1832 (Engels' note).

Bridge, the passer-by sees several ruined walls and heaps of debris with some newer houses. The view from this bridge, mercifully concealed from mortals of small stature by a parapet as high as a man, is characteristic for the whole district. At the bottom flows, or rather stagnates, the Irk, a narrow, coal-black, foul-smelling stream, full of debris and refuse, which it deposits on the shallower right bank. In dry weather, a long string of the most disgusting, blackish-green, slime pools are left standing on this bank, from the depths of which bubbles of miasmic gas constantly arise and give forth a stench unendurable even on the bridge forty or fifty feet above the surface of the stream. But besides this, the stream itself is checked every few paces by high weirs, behind which slime and refuse accumulate and rot in thick masses. Above the bridge are tanneries, bonemills, and gasworks, from which all drains and refuse find their way into the Irk, which receives further the contents of all the neighbouring sewers and privies. It may easily be imagined, therefore, what sort of residue the stream deposits. Below the bridge you look upon the piles of debris, the refuse, filth and offal from the courts on the steep left bank; here each house is packed close behind its neighbour and a piece of each is visible, all black, smoky, crumbling, ancient, with broken panes and window frames. The background is furnished by old barrack-like factory buildings. On the lower right bank stands a long row of houses and mills; the second house being a ruin without a roof, piled with debris; the third house stands so low that the lowest floor is uninhabitable and therefore without windows or doors.[2]

The New Town stretches up a hill of clay, beyond the Old Town, between the Irk and St. George's Road. Here all the features of a city are lost. Single rows of houses or groups of streets stand, here and there, like little villages on the naked, not even grass-grown clay soil; the houses, or rather cottages, are in bad order, never repaired, filthy, with damp, unclean cellar dwellings; the lanes are neither paved nor supplied with sewers, but harbour numerous colonies of swine penned in small sties or yards, or wandering unrestrained through the neighbourhood. The mud in the streets is so deep that there is never a chance, except in the driest weather, of walking without sinking into it ankle deep at every step. In the vicinity of St. George's Road, the separate groups of buildings approach each other more closely, ending in a continuation of lanes, blind alleys, back lanes and courts, which

[2] F. Engels, *Condition of the Working Classes in England in 1844*, tr. Florence Kelly Wischnewetzky, reprinted London, 1952, pp. 48–50.

grow more and more crowded and irregular the nearer they approach the heart of the town. True, they are here oftener paved or supplied with paved sidewalks and gutters; but the filth, the bad order of the houses, and especially of the cellars, remains the same.

It may not be out of place to make some general observations just here as to the customary construction of working-men's quarters in Manchester. We have seen how in the Old Town pure accident determined the grouping of the houses in general. Every house is built without reference to any other, and the scraps of space between them are called courts for want of another name. In the somewhat newer portions of the same quarter, and in other working-men's quarters, a somewhat more orderly arrangement may be found. The space between two streets is divided into more regular, usually square courts, more or less as follows:

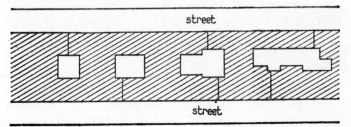

street

street

17 Diagram showing how the space between two streets has been divided into courts.

they were built in this way from the beginning, and communicate with the streets by means of covered passages. If the totally planless construction is injurious to the health of the workers by preventing ventilation, this method of shutting them up in courts surrounded on all sides by buildings is far more so. The air simply cannot escape; the chimneys of the houses are the sole drains for the imprisoned atmosphere of the courts, and they serve the purpose only as long as a fire is kept burning. Moreover, the houses surrounding such courts are usually built back to back, having the rear wall in common; and this alone suffices to prevent any sufficient through ventilation. And, as the police charged with the care of the streets, does not trouble itself about the condition of these courts, as everything lies quietly where it is thrown, there is no cause for wonder at the filth and heaps of ashes and offal to be found here. I have been in courts, in Millers Street, at least half a foot below the level of the thoroughfare and without the slightest drainage for that water that accumulated in them in rainy weather! More recently another different method of building was adopted, and has now become general. Working-men's cottages are almost never built singly, but always by the dozen or score; a single contractor building up one or two streets at a time. These are then arranged as follows: One front is formed of cottages of the best class, so fortunate as to possess a back door and small court, and these command the highest rent. In the rear of these cottages runs a narrow alley, the back street, built up at both ends, into which either a narrow roadway or a covered passage leads from one side. The cottages which face this back street command least rent and are most neglected. These have their rear walls in common with the third row of cottages which face a second street, and command less rent than the first row and more than the second.

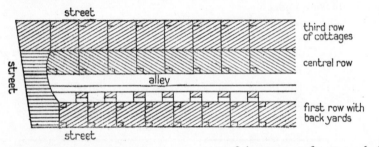

18 Diagram showing the arrangement of three rows of cottages built by a single contracter.

By this method of construction, comparatively good ventilation can be obtained for the first row of cottages, and the third row is no worse off than in the former method. The middle row, on the other hand, is at least as badly ventilated as the houses in the courts, and the back street is always in the same filthy, disgusting condition as they. The contractors prefer this method because it saves them space, and furnishes the means of fleecing better paid workers through the higher rents of the cottages in the first and third rows. These three different forms of cottage building are found all over Manchester and throughout Lancashire and Yorkshire, often mixed up together, but usually separate enough to indicate the relative ages of parts of towns. The third system, that of back alleys, prevails largely in the great working-men's district east of St. George's Road and Ancoats Street, and is the one most often found in the other working-men's quarters of Manchester and its suburbs.

In the last-mentioned broad district included under the name

Ancoats, stand the largest mills of Manchester lining the canals, colossal six- or seven-storied buildings towering with their slender chimneys far above the low cottages of the workers. The population of the district consists, therefore, chiefly of mill-hands and, in the worst streets, of hand-weavers. The streets nearest the heart of the town are the oldest, and consequently the worst; they are, however, paved and supplied with drains. Among them I include those nearest to and parallel with Oldham Road and Great Ancoats Street. Farther to the north-east lie many newly-built-up streets; here the cottages look neat and cleanly, doors and windows are new and freshly painted, the rooms within newly whitewashed; the streets themselves are better aired, the vacant buildings lots between them larger and more numerous. But this can be said of a minority of the houses only, while cellar dwellings are to be found under almost every cottage; many streets are unpaved and without sewers; and, worse than all, this neat appearance is all pretence which vanishes within the first ten years. For the construction of the cottages individually is no less to be condemned than the plan of the streets. All such cottages look neat and substantial at first; their massive brick walls deceive the eye, and, on passing through a newly-built working-men's street, without remembering the back-alleys and the construction of the houses themselves, one is inclined to agree with the assertion of the Liberal manufacturers that the working population is nowhere so well housed as in England. But on closer examination, it becomes evident that the walls of these cottages are as thin as it is possible to make them. The outer walls, those of the cellar, which bear the weight of the ground floor and roof, are one whole brick thick at most, the bricks lying with their long sides touching; but I have seen many a cottage of the same height, some in process of building, whose outer walls were but one half brick thick, lying not sidewise but lengthwise, their narrow ends touching. The object of this is to spare material, but there is also another reason for it; namely, the fact that the contractors never own the land but lease it, according to the English custom, for twenty, thirty, forty, fifty or nine-nine years, at the expiration of which time it falls, with everything upon it, back into the possession of the original holder, who pays nothing in return for improvements upon it. The improvements are therefore so calculated by the lessee as to be worth as little as possible at the expiration of the stipulated term. And as such cottages are often built but twenty or thirty years before the expiration of the term, it may easily be imagined that the contractors make no unnecessary expenditures upon them. Moreover, these contractors, usually carpenters and builders, or manufacturers, spend little or nothing in repairs, partly to avoid diminishing their rent receipts, and partly in view of the approaching surrender of the improvement to the landowner; while in consequence of commercial crises and the loss of work that follows them, whole streets often stand empty, the cottages falling rapidly into ruin and uninhabitableness.[3]

There follows a description of one of these dilapidated cottage quarters:

In a rather deep hole, in a curve of the Medlock and surrounded on all four sides by tall factories and high embankments, covered with buildings, stand two groups of about two hundred cottages, built chiefly back to back, in which live about four thousand human beings, most of them Irish. The cottages are old, dirty, and of the smallest sort, the streets uneven, fallen into ruts and in part without drains or pavement; masses of refuse, offal and sickening filth lie among standing pools in all directions; the atmosphere is poisoned by the effluvia from these, and ladened and darkened by the smoke of a dozen tall factory chimneys. A horde of ragged women and children swarm about here, as filthy as the swine that thrive upon the garbage heaps and in the puddles. In short, the whole rookery furnishes such a hateful and repulsive spectacle as can hardly be equalled in the worst court on the Irk. The race that lives in these ruinous cottages, behind broken windows, mended with oilskin, sprung doors and rotten door-posts, or in dark, wet cellars, in measureless filth and stench, in this atmosphere penned in as if with a purpose, this race must really have reached the lowest stage of humanity. This is the impression and the line of thought which the exterior of this district forces upon the beholder. But what must one think when he hears that in each of these pens, containing at most two rooms, a garret and perhaps a cellar, on the average twenty human beings live; that in the whole region, for each one hundred and twenty persons, one usually inaccessible privy is provided; and that in spite of the excitement into which the cholera epidemic plunged the sanitary police by reason of the condition of Little Ireland, in spite of everything, in the year of grace 1844, it is in almost the same state as in 1831! Dr. Kay asserts that not only the cellars but the first floors of all the houses in this district are damp; that a number of cellars once filled up with earth have now been

[3] Ibid., pp. 54-8.

emptied and are occupied once more by Irish people; that in one cellar the water constantly wells up through a hole stopped with clay, the cellar lying below the river level, so that its occupant, a handloom weaver, had to bale out the water from his dwelling every morning and pour it into the street![4]

Engels was describing the worst cases, not the average. Yet his collection of extreme cases is justified in that public opinion no longer considered them acceptable, independently of the fact that they were so common and widespread. This was the real starting point for their censure in contemporary literature and for subsequent reforming action.

The hardships of pre-industrial society were regarded as part of an unavoidable destiny which had existed since time immemorial and seemed, at least within the span of a single generation, substantially unalterable. But the industrial town was something new, something which had grown up during a limited period of time under the eyes of those people who were now experiencing its discomforts. This was a unique phenomenon that shook contemporary habits and concepts, but which seemed the reverse of being preordained and inevitable. There did not yet exist a rational system for controlling the mechanisms of this growth, but it seemed natural that the inventive powers of man and the strength of machines should be able to change the course of the situation which they themselves had created.

Every age had known conditions as bad as, and possibly worse than, those described by Engels and other writers of the early nineteenth century, and it is possible to counter their descriptions with other, earlier ones such as those by Vauban (1698), Boisguillebeit (1697) and Mercier (1783) which repeat the same criticisms almost word for word. In fact the difference does not lie in the details described, but in the tone of the descriptions: gloomy and resigned in pre-industrial writings, later they become full of the spirit of change and brightened, despite the squalor of the present, by a faith in a better future.

[4] *Ibid.*, pp. 60-1.

Poverty, a condition which had been borne for centuries without hope of a reasonable alternative, was now recognized as an extreme condition of hardship, in other words it was now seen as an evil which could and should be eliminated by every available means.

Aneurin Bevan writes:

> By poverty I mean the general consciousness of unnecessary deprivation, which is the normal state of millions of people in modern industrial society, accompanied by a deep sense of frustration and dissatisfaction with the existing state of social affairs. It is no answer to say that things are better than they were. People live in the present, not in the past. Discontent arises from a knowledge of the possible, as contrasted with the actual. There is a universal and justifiable conviction that the lot of the ordinary man and woman is much worse than it need be.[5]

The origins of modern town-planning are thus to be sought at that moment in time when circumstances had crystallized sufficiently not only to cause the discomfort but also to provoke the protest of the people involved. Historical discussion must at this point extend beyond such matters as the patterns of settlement to embrace the social problems of the time, thus demonstrating how modern town-planning should be regarded as an integral part of the general attempt to extend the potential benefits of the Industrial Revolution to members of all classes, and emphasizing the inevitable political implications inherent in what might appear to be a purely technical field.

It was not by chance that the first important incident in the history of nineteenth-century social conflict should have occurred in Manchester, in 1819: the Peterloo episode.

The government's repressive policies had forced workers' associations and radical extremists to act together. The workers were reading Cobbett's *Political Register*, which had been available for twopence since 1816, and the government was reacting by mobilizing the army and police, by ordering preventive

[5] A. Bevan, *In Place of Fear*, London, 1961, p. 22.

arrests and suspending the age-old safeguard of habeas corpus.

On 16 August 1819 ... an orderly and unarmed crowd of about sixty thousand men, women and children was permitted to assemble; but then the magistrates, stricken with alarm at the sight of so great a multitude, sent in the yeomanry to arrest the speaker, the notorious Radical Hunt, after the meeting had fairly begun. When the horsemen, pushing their way through the throng on such an errand, were shouted at and hustled, the cavalry in reserve were ordered by the magistrates to charge. Their impact drove the dense mass of human beings, cursing and shrieking, off the field, while the yeomanry, who were Tory partisans, used their sabres with gusto. In the disturbances of that day some eleven people, including two women, were killed or died of their injuries; over one hundred were wounded by sabres and several hundred more injured by horse-hoofs or crushed in the stampede. The women injured were over a hundred.[6]

This episode fired the contemporary imagination and became known as the Peterloo massacre. History has confirmed its importance, and the name Peterloo follows that of Waterloo in all history books, emphasizing the contrast between the glories of foreign policy and the gloom of affairs at home.

Contemporaries were struck not so much by the facts themselves nor by the cruelty of the magistrates responsible, who clearly gave way to panic instead of keeping to a pre-arranged plan, but by the utter futility of the behaviour of both parties who appeared to have reached an absolute deadlock.

The authorities could not reasonably hope for any lasting result from their high handedness (English history had long since made it impossible to govern by such means), while the demonstrators, inhabitants of the yards and allays described by Engels, were fired by a strong spirit of rebellion, although they had not as yet fully defined their aims.

Cobbett had invented one very significant catchword: the 'Thing', to indicate 'the union of Ministers, borough-mongers, pensioners, squires, clergy and manufacturers, by which he con-

[6] G. M. Trevelyan, *British History in the Nineteenth Century*, London, 1922, p. 189.

ceived England to be bound, bullied and bled';[7] it was against such an image that the people of Peterloo, as yet unable to fix their sights on more precise objectives, had protested.

Thus the awareness of the discomforts of the industrial town and the protests of its inhabitants existed within an ideological vacuum which left the society of the first decades of the nineteenth century momentarily devoid of the means to do anything practical about righting the evils of which it complained; the old methods were inadequate and discredited, new ones had not yet emerged.

From this time on the problem was to fill this void with a series of individual actions, proposals and laws which could harden into a new, logical body of experience; to define the features of the 'Thing' one by one, prior to successfully modifying them.

Modern town-planning is not merely an attempt to represent this process in visual terms, by transposing its application to the problems of the use of space, but must also be regarded as a vital factor in the creation of a democratic society. Viewed in this way, town-planning loses both the position of apparent detachment from social problems which it had hitherto occupied in the shadow of absolute power, and its apparent ability to regulate the balance of the various forms of community ideally and definitively. It appears in a more humble guise as one of the techniques necessary to determine this balance and its aim is no longer the instant achievement of formal perfection, but a series of partial alterations, a reasonable compromise between the forces involved, a compromise which varies continually according to the changing relationships of these forces.

In the years between 1815 and 1848, from Waterloo to the February Revolution, the technical and the political aspects of thought and research in the field of town-planning were very closely, almost inextricably, connected.

This is typical of the culture of the time, as exemplified by the case of Jeremy Bentham, the Radical philosopher who put the

[7] *Ibid.*, p. 187.

best years of his life, and a large part of his inheritance, into realizing his 'Panopticon', a model prison built in such a way that only one gaoler was needed to supervise all the prisoners, by means of a system of mirrors that enabled him to see them without them seeing him.

The pronounced tendency to associate the technical and the ideological in town-planning seems disconcerting and ingenuous to us today, in that it was based upon an inaccurate assessment of the forces involved and of the real difficulties to be overcome, which were to reveal themselves gradually as time went on. Nonetheless this capacity for association was a productive source of inspiration, and it bore witness to the ideal unity underlying the various nineteenth-century experiments even when, after 1848, they began to reveal remarkable diversity among themselves.

Thus this period, though in terms of actual achievement it was in a sense the pre-history of town-planning, was extremely important in that it saw the formation of various fundamental theories.

From this moment onwards the dual nature, scientific and moralistic, of town-planning, is constantly emphasized, and it was soon clear that the particular combination of motives of these early planners was going to distinguish their essentially responsible action sharply from the dependent, literary and ambiguous attitude of writers of earlier times. This new attitude can be summed up in Brecht's words:

> Contempt and tenacity, knowledge and rebellion,
> understanding of the part and of the whole.[8]

Within this sphere there existed two possible, and for the moment completely separate, courses of action. The problems of modern town-planning could be approached either by drawing up, as an alternative to the existing towns, a complete ideological model, to be created, experimentally, de novo and independently from the original it set out to correct, or by tackling the various

[8] B. Brecht, *The Measures Taken*, 1931.

BUILDING AND FURNITURE

FOR AN

INDUSTRY-HOUSE ESTABLISHMENT,

FOR 2000 PERSONS, OF ALL AGES.

ON THE

PANOPTICON OR CENTRAL-INSPECTION PRINCIPLE.

—————

☞ For the Explanation of the several Figures of this PLATE, see "Outline of a Work, entitled PAUPER MANAGEMENT IMPROVED;" Bentham's Works, vol. viii., p. 369 to p. 439.

The Ranges of Bed-Stages and Cribs are respectively supposed to run from End to End of the *radial* Walls, as exhibited in the GROUND PLAN: they are here represented as cut through by a Line parallel to the Side of the Polygon: in the Bed-Stages, what is represented as *one* in the Draught, is proposed to be in *two* in the Description.

FIG. I.—ELEVATION.

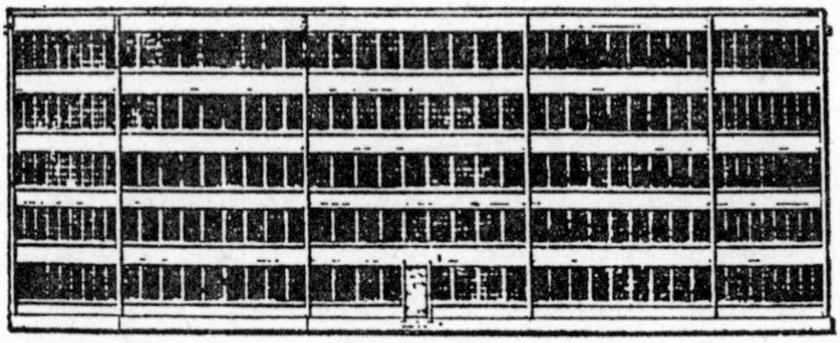

Figure 25a

19 (A and B)   Bentham's Panopticon.

36

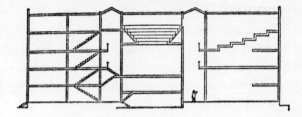

FIG. II.—SECTION

FIG. III.—GROUND PLAN.

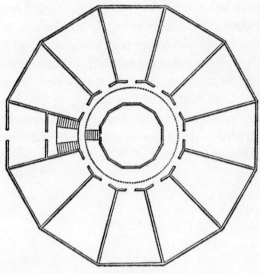

Figure 25b

technical needs connected with the growth of the industrial town and attempting to cure its individual defects.

These two courses tended to converge since attempts at putting theoretical models into practise brought these theories into sharp contact with reality, while provisions for dealing with single technical problems emphasized the links between these different problems and threw into relief the underlying question of the planned use of land.

For this reason this work is divided into two parts: in the first of these I will discuss nineteenth-century Utopias—those of Owen, St. Simon, Fourier and Cabet—and the attempts to put them into practice and in the second I shall examine the theoretical experiments which upset the traditional balance between the various uses to which land was put and which therefore created the need for a new and carefully calculated equilibrium. As we shall see, the main impulse did not come from large-scale public works, but from minor sanitary defects in the large industrial towns, depending on a large number of factors and necessitating special legislation that soon spread from sanitation to the field of town-planning in general.

1 nineteenth-century utopias

OWEN AND THE ENGLISH CO-OPERATIVE MOVEMENT

Robert Owen (1771–1858) began to earn his living at the age of ten as a shop assistant in London. In 1789 he set up a small weaving business and was so successful that, ten years later, he was able, with several partners, to buy up the spinning-mills of New Lanark in Scotland.

He became a member, in 1793, of the Literary and Philosophical Society of Manchester, where he met Dalton and was probably influenced by Dr. Perceval, one of the first promoters of factory legislation. It has also been suggested that he was influenced by Thomas Spence (1750–1814), one of the radical philosophers persecuted by the government during the period of anti-Jacobin reaction. Yet his convictions, based on his personal experience as a worker and later as a leading industrialist, were strikingly original in his own time for he realized that the 'self-made man' postulated by economists and accepted by current opinion was a mere abstraction, since for the most part environmental conditions determined individual destinies. In order to improve the

39

lot of the individual the reformer had therefore to start with the environment, which must be recreated in order to favour the individual before thought was given to any economic advantage, whether individual or collective.

Owen put this idea to the test in the mills at New Lanark, where he introduced a series of improvements in the treatment of his workers: better pay, shorter hours, better housing and, in 1816, the unique 'Institution for the Formation of Character'.

The Institution—said Owen in his inaugural address—has been devised to afford the means of receiving your children at an early age, as soon almost as they can walk. (. . .) The middle room of the lower storey will be appropriated to their accommodation; and in this their chief occupation will be to play and amuse themselves in severe weather: at other times they will be permitted to occupy the enclosed area before the building; for to give children a vigorous constitution, they ought to be kept as much as possible in the open air. As they advance in years, they will be taken into the rooms on the right and left, where they will be regularly instructed in the rudiments of common learning; which, before they shall be six years old, they may be taught in a superior manner. When your children have passed through these stages, they will be admitted into this place (intended also to be used as a chapel) which, with the adjoining apartment, is to be the general schoolroom for reading, writing, arithmetic, sewing and knitting; all which, on the plan to be pursued, will be accomplished to a considerable extent by the time the children are ten years old; before which age, none of them will be permitted to enter the works.

For the benefit of the health and spirits of the children both boys and girls will be taught to dance, and the boys instructed in military exercises; those of each sex who may have good voices will be taught to sing, and those among the boys who have a taste for music will be taught to play upon some instrument; for it is intended to give them as much diversified innocent amusement as the local circumstances of the establishment will admit.

The rooms to the east and west on the storey below, will also be appropriated in bad weather for relaxation and exercise during some part of the day, to the children who, in the regular hours of teaching, are to be instructed in these apartments.

In this manner is the Institution to be occupied during the day in winter. In summer, it is intended that they shall derive knowledge from a personal examination of the works of nature and of art, by going out frequently with some of their masters into the neighbourhood and country around.

After the instruction of the children who are too young to attend the works shall have been finished for the day, the apartments shall be cleaned, ventilated and in winter lighted and heated, and in all respects made comfortable, for the reception of the other classes of the population. The apartments on this floor are then to be appropriated for the use of the children and youth of both sexes who have been employed at work during the day, and who may wish to improve themselves in reading, writing, arithmetic, sewing, or knitting; or to learn any of the useful arts; to instruct them in which, proper masters and mistresses, who are appointed, will attend for two hours every evening.

The three lower rooms, which in winter will also be well-lighted and properly heated, will be thrown open for the use of the adult part of the population, who are to be provided with every accommodation requisite to enable them to read, write, account, sew, or play, converse or walk about. . . .

Two evenings in the week will be appropriated to dancing and music: but on these occasions every accommodation will be prepared for those who prefer to study or to follow any of the occupations pursued on the other evenings. One of the apartments will also be occasionally appropriated for the purpose of giving useful instruction to the older classes of the inhabitants. . . .

I wish to benefit all equally; but circumstances limit my present measures for the public good within a narrow circle. I must begin to act at some point; and a combination of singular events has fixed that point at this establishment. The first and greatest advantages therefore centre here. But, in unison with the principle thus stated, it has ever been my intention that this Institution, when completed, will accommodate more than the children of parents resident at the village, any persons living at Lanark, or in the neighbourhood anywhere around, who cannot well afford to educate their children, shall be at liberty, on mentioning their wishes, to send them to this place, where they will experience the same care and attention as those who belong to the establishment.[9]

This speech, made in 1816, is of the greatest possible interest:

[9] R. Owen, 'An Address to the Inhabitants of New Lanark, Delivered on Opening the Institution for the Formation of Character, on the 1st of January 1816 (in *A New View of Society and Other Writings,* London, 1927, pp. 98–101).

here for the first time a philanthropic enterprise was taking the form of a permanent educational organization and, with this as its starting point, was beginning to affect the lives of the entire community, complementing work in the factory with study and leisure, and allotting suitable accommodation, and time, to each activity.

The capitalist economy and the new techniques of factory work shattered the old patterns of living, producing evils and miseries which were felt all over England. Yet these same techniques and this same capacity for organization could be extended from labour to the other aspects of life, from the factory to the town, and theoretically it was possible to conceive of a reversal of the present process of disintegration, produced as it was by a one-sided application of these principles.

The Institution and other amenities established by Owen in New Lanark worked extremely well for several years. But the very nature of Owen's thesis was that they should have wider application and the following year, in his Report to the Committee on the Poor Laws, he put forward his Utopia as the universal remedy for the problem of poverty as it then existed.[10]

Why, he enquired, was there unemployment?

At the end of the war England had 'a productive power, which operated to the same effect as if her population had actually increased fifteen or twenty fold'. But, when war production ceased, 'the revenues of the world were inadequate to purchase that which a power so enormous in its effects did produce: a diminished demand consequently followed. When therefore it became necessary to contract the sources of supply, it soon proved that mechanical power was much cheaper than human labour; the former, in consequence, was continued at work, while the latter was superseded; and human labour may now be obtained at a price far less than is absolutely necessary for the subsistence of the individual in ordinary comfort.'

[10] R. Owen, 'Report to the Committee for the Relief of the Manufacturing Poor, March 1817 (in *A New View of Society and Other Writings*, pp. 157–64).

Therefore, as long as human labour and machines were considered on the same level, 'the working classes had no adequate means of contending with mechanical power; one of three results must therefore ensue:

(*i*) the use of mechanism must be greatly diminished; or
(*ii*) millions of human beings must be starved, to permit its existence to the present extent; or
(*iii*) advantageous occupation must be found for the poor and unemployed working-classes, to whose labour mechanism must be rendered subservient, instead of being applied, as at present, to supersede it.'

Owen showed that the third possibility was the only reasonable one, and formulated the aims of the inevitable reforming action as follows: to find 'advantageous occupation . . . for the unemployed working classes, under an arrangement which will permit mechanical improvements to be carried out to any extent.'

After establishing this political premise—which corresponded with the beginnings of modern socialism—Owen proceeded to describe his plan as follows:

. . . any plan for the amelioration of the poor should combine means to prevent their children from acquiring bad habits, and to give them good ones—to provide useful training and instruction for them—to provide proper labour for the adults—to direct their labour and expenditure so as to produce the greatest benefit to themselves and to society; and to place them under such circumstances as shall remove them from unnecessary temptations, and closely unite their interest and duty.

These advantages cannot be given either to individuals or to families separately, or to large congregated numbers. They can be effectually introduced into practice only under arrangements that would unite in one establishment a population of from five hundred to one thousand five hundred persons, averaging about one thousand. . . .

The drawing exhibits, in the foreground, an establishment, with its appendages and appropriate quantity of land; and at due distances, other villages of a similar description.

Squares of buildings are here represented sufficient to accommodate

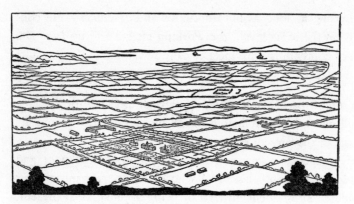

20 Drawing of Robert Owen's ideal Village.

about 1,200 persons each; and surrounded by a quantity of land, from 1,000 to 1,500 acres. Within the squares are public buildings, which divide them into paralellograms.

The central building contains a public kitchen, mess-rooms and all the accommodation necessary to economical and comfortable cooking and eating. To the right of this is a building, of which the ground-floor will form the infant school, and the other a lecture-room and a place of worship. The building to the left contains a school for the older children, and a committee room on the ground floor; above, a library and a room for adults. In the vacant space between the squares are enclosed grounds for exercise and recreation: these enclosures are supposed to have trees planted in them.

It is intended that three sides of each square shall be lodging houses, chiefly for the married, consisting of four rooms in each: each room to be sufficiently large to house a man, his wife, and two children. The fourth side is designed for dormitories for all the children exceeding two in a family, or above three years of age. In the centre of this square are apartments for those who superintend the dormitories: at one extremity of it the infirmary; and at the other a building for the accommodation of strangers who may come from a distance to see their friends or relatives. In the centre of two sides of the squares are apartments for general superintendents, clergymen, schoolmasters, surgeons etc.; and in the third are store-rooms for all the articles required for the use of the establishment. On the outside, and at the back of the houses around the squares, are gardens, bounded by roads. Immediately, beyond these, on one side, are buildings for mechanical and manufac-

44

turing purposes. The slaughter-house, stabling etc., to be separated from the establishment by plantations. At the other side are offices for washing, bleaching etc.; and at a still greater distance from the squares, are some of the farming establishments, with conveniences for malting, brewing, and corn-mills etc.; around these are cultivated enclosures, pasture-land etc., the hedgerows of which are planted with fruit-trees. . . .

Each lodging-room within the square is to accommodate a man, his wife and two children under the age of three years; and to be such as will permit them to have much more comforts than the dwellings of the poor usually afford.

It is intended that the children above three years of age should attend the school, eat in the mess-room and sleep in the dormitories; the parents being, of course, permitted to see and converse with them at meals and all other proper times; that before they leave school they shall be well instructed in all necessary and useful knowledge; that every possible means shall be adopted to prevent the acquirement of bad habits from their parents or otherwise; that no pains shall be spared to impress upon them such habits and dispositions as may be most conducive to their happiness through life, as well as render them useful and valuable members of the community to which they belong.

It is proposed that the women be employed:
First: in the care of their infants, and in keeping their dwellings in the best order.
Second: in cultivating the gardens to raise vegetables for the supply of the public kitchen.
Third: in attending to such of the branches of the various manufactures as women can well undertake; but not to be employed more than four or five hours a day.
Fourth: in making up clothing for the inmates of the establishment.
Fifth: in attending occasionally, and in rotation, in the public kitchen, mess-rooms, and dormitories; and, when properly instructed, in superintending some parts of the education of the children in the schools.

It is proposed that the elder children should be trained to assist in gardening and manufacturing for a portion of the day, according to their strength; and that the men should be employed, all of them, in agriculture, and also in manufactures, or some other occupation for the benefit of the establishment.

The ignorance of the poor, their ill-training, and their want of a

45

rational education make it necessary that those of the present generation should be actively and regularly occupied through the day in some essentially useful work; yet in such a manner as their employment shall be healthy and productive. The plan which has been described will amply permit of this.

In order to offer some practical idea of the expenses that would be incurred in founding such an establishment for 1,200 souls, the following items are submitted. If the land be purchased:

1,200 acres of land at £30 per acre	£36,000
Lodging apartments for 1,200 persons	£17,000
Three public buildings within the square	£11,000
Manufactory, slaughter house and washing-house	£9,000
Furnishing 300 lodging rooms, at £8 each	£2,400
Furnishing kitchen, school and dormitories	£3,000
Two farming establishments, with corn-mill and malting and brewing appendages	£5,000
Making the interior of the square and roads	£3,000
Stock for the farm under spade cultivation	£4,000
Contingencies and extras	£6,600
	£96,000

This sum, being divided by 1,200, gives a capital to be advanced of £80 per head; or, at five per cent per annum, £4 each per year.

This plan was discussed more fully in an address to the authorities of the County of Lanark, in 1820.[11]

The first part of the document consists of a piece of economic reasoning, based on the following premises:

First: that manual labour, properly directed, is the source of all wealth, and of national prosperity.

Second: that, when properly directed, labour is of far more value to the community than the expense necessary to maintain the labourer in considerable comfort.

Third: that manual labour, properly directed, may be made to continue of this value in all parts of the world, under any supposable increase of its population, for many centuries to come.

Fourth: that, under a proper direction of manual labour, Great Britain

[11] R. Owen, 'Report to the County of Lanark, 1st of May, 1820' (in *A New View of Society and Other Writings*, p. 276).

and its dependencies may be made to support an incalculable increase of population, most advantageously for all its inhabitants.

Fifth: that when manual labour shall be so directed, it will be found that population cannot, for many years, be stimulated to 'advance as rapidly as society might be benefitted by its increase'.

Therefore, if poverty and unemployment do exist, 'some formidable artificial obstacle must have intervened to obstruct the natural improvement and progress of society'.

This obstacle was not natural, but was connected with the speed at which the transformations were taking place: in Owen's view, 'the want of beneficial employment for the working classes and the consequent public distress were owing to the rapid increase of the new productive power, for the advantageous application of which society had neglected to make the proper arrangements.'

This thesis, inverting as it did the Malthusian reasoning hitherto commonly accepted, was stated in strictly economic terms:

(*i*) It must be admitted that scientific or artificial aids to man increase his productive powers, his natural wants remaining the same; and in proportion as his productive powers increase he becomes less dependent on his physical strength and on the many contingencies connected with it.

(*ii*) That the direct effect of every addition to scientific, or mechanical and chemical power is to increase wealth; and it is found, accordingly, that the immediate cause of the present want of employment for the working classes is an excess of production of all kinds of wealth by which, under the existing arrangements of commerce, all the markets of the world are overstocked.

(*iii*) That, if markets could be found, an incalculable addition might yet be made to the wealth of society, as is most evident from the number of persons who seek employment, and the far greater number who, from ignorance, are inefficiently employed, but still more from the means we possess of increasing, to an unlimited extent, our scientific powers of production.

(*iv*) That the deficiency of employment for the working classes cannot proceed from want of wealth or capital, or of the means of greatly adding to that which now exists, but from some defect in the mode of distributing this extraordinary addition of new capital throughout society, or, to speak commercially, from the want of a market, or means of exchange, co-extensive with the means of production.

It is from this that the two main points of Owen's economic programme derive: the adoption of human labour as the unit for measuring value, and the creation of an internal market, thus increasing the workers' profits so as to enable them to be consumers of the goods produced and not mere instruments of production.

This necessitated various changes in organization; the most important concerned the tilling of the soil, which Owen wanted done with the spade rather than the plough and which was to be the main occupation of the whole population. The next problem —which brings him to the subject of town-planning—is the following: 'how were these new cultivators to be placed on the soil and associated, that their exertions may have the most beneficial result for themselves and the community?'

Point by point, as elsewhere, Owen defined the characteristics of the new establishments:

(*i*) The number of persons who were to associate to form the nucleus of the new society might vary between a minimum of 300 to a maximum of 2,000, being preferably between 800 and 1,200.

(*ii*) The land to be cultivated by the community 'will probably be half an acre to an acre and a half for each individual; an association of 1,200 persons would require from 600–1,800 statute acres.'

(*iii*) The description of the residential centre is similar to that of 1817; all the buildings were to be grouped round a great square in the shape of a parallelogram; the four sides would be occupied by accommodation for the adults, by the common dormitories for the children, store-rooms, guest-rooms and infirmary; the central building would house the church, school, kitchens and refectory.

As it is of essential importance that there should be abundance of space within the line of the private dwellings, the parallelogram, in all cases, whether the association is to be near the intended maximum or

48

the minimum in numbers, should be of large dimensions; and to accommodate a greater or less population, the private dwellings should be of one, two, three or four storeys, and the interior arrangements formed accordingly.

These will be very simple. No kitchen will be necessary, as the public arrangements for cooking will supersede the necessity of any. The apartments will always be well-ventilated and, when necessary, heated or cooled on the improved principles lately introduced in the Derby Infirmary. To heat, cool and ventilate the apartments, the parties will have no further trouble than to open or shut two slides, or valves, in each room, the atmosphere of which, by this simple contrivance, may always be kept temperate and pure.

One stove of proper dimensions, judiciously placed, will supply the apartments of several dwellings, with very little trouble and at a very little expense, when the buildings are originally adapted for this arrangement. . . . good sleeping apartments looking over the gardens in the country, and sitting rooms of proper dimensions fronting on to the square, will afford as much lodging-accommodation as, with the other public arrangements, can be useful to, or desired by, these associated lodgers.

For the children's education this time Owen suggested two schools, one for 'infants from two to six years of age, the second for children from six to twelve'.

The gardens, as implied, were to be situated outside the parallelogram 'and, beyond them, at a sufficient distance to be covered by a plantation, should be placed the workshops and manufactory'.

Owen himself compares his parallelogram to a machine and concludes: 'if the invention of various machines has multiplied the power of labour, in several instances, to the apparent advantage of particular individuals, while it has deteriorated the condition of many others, this is an invention which will at once multiply the physical and mental powers of the whole society to an incalculable extent, without injuring any one by its introduction or its most rapid diffusion.'[12]

This proposal of Owen's is the first piece of modern town-planning to be worked out in every detail, from the political and

[12] *Ibid.*, pp. 285–6.

economic premises to the actual building plans and financial estimate.

The public was interested but above all amazed and disconcerted by Owen's plan. He himself published several explanatory articles in the *London Newspaper* in 1817[13] and put his programme forward at two public meetings in London in the August of the same year. He received encouragement from the government and the press, as well as the approval of economists such as Ricardo, but he was criticized by most specialists, including Malthus, Cobbett and Place.

Peacock caricatured Owen, under the name of Mr. Toogood, as the 'co-operationist . . . who wants to parcel out the world into squares like a chess-board, with a community on each, raising everything for one another, with a steam engine . . . like a maid of all work.'[14]

What invalidated Owen's reasoning in the eyes of the specialists of the time was his inversion of the usual economic terms—hence the concept of the steam engine as the maid of all work, rather than as an instrument to increase industrial productivity.

For us today Owen's plan appears important precisely because it contains this first hint of awareness of the organizational difficulties produced by mechanical progress and because it marks the beginning of the new line of thought from which modern town-planning was gradually to emerge. On the other hand, we can see its weak points clearly because we are in a position to measure the immense abyss between his simple formulation and the infinitely more complex problems posed by subsequent developments. To take a specific point, Owen was so absorbed in his outline of the new organization space and of society, with his preachings about casting off the shackles created by the old order, that he completely overlooked the problem of authority and individual freedom.

Describing the means of actually realizing his parallelograms to

[13] *London Newspaper* of 30 July, 15 August, 19 August, 22 August and 10 Sept. 1817
[14] Quoted in B. Russell, *Freedom and Organization, 1814-1914*, London, 1934, p. 185.

the authorities of the County of Lanark, Owen limited himself to saying:

these new farming and general working arrangements may be formed by one or any number of landed proprietors or large capitalists; by established companies having large funds to expend for benevolent and public objects; by parishes and counties, to relieve themselves from paupers and poor-rates; and by associations of the middle and working classes of farmers, mechanics and tradesmen, to relieve themselves from the evils of the present system. . . . the new establishments would remain subject to the central government of the country and would pay its taxes in the legal circulating medium (though internally they would be using the new labour notes), and would furnish soldiers in times of war; but in return they would make no claims upon the country's system of justice because, having achieved perfect harmony, they would be in no need of courts or prisons.[15]

The attempted transition from theory to practice soon revealed the weaknesses of Owen's plan; he laid his proposals before all the great people of his time, before the future Tzar Nicholas I on a visit to New Lanark, before Napoleon I on Elba, before the Emperor of Russia, Alexander I, during the Congress of Aix-la-Chapelle as well as before the government of his own country.[16]

But the failure of all these proposals encouraged him to make a personal attempt at putting them into practice and in 1825 he purchased 30,000 acres from a Protestant sect in Indiana and settled there in 1826 with his family and a group of about 800 followers, all eager to bring about immediate universal harmony.

The decision to emigrate to America evolved from the tendency to consider the New World as an open field for experiments which were impossible in Europe. It was also linked with the recent experiments of the Napoleonic veterans who had gone to America after Waterloo to build their Champ d'Asyle, and of the German religious reformers, such as George Rapp who had founded the village of Harmony which Owen later bought.[17]

[15] 'Report to the County of Lanark,' *cit.,* p. 285.
[16] B. Russell, *op. cit.,* p. 188.
[17] R. W. Leopold (*Robert Owen, a Biography*, Cambridge, 1940, p. 25) quotes a hymn sung by Owen's followers in 1825, which begins as follows:
'Land of the West, we fly to thee,
Sick of the old world's sophistry.'

E

This village, renamed New Harmony, had been designed like a chessboard with a central square surrounded by large brick buildings. The Duke of Saxe-Weimar, who visited it in 1826, describes it as follows:

Mr. Owen was glad of my visit and offered to show me everything. ... As the arrangement calculated for Rapp's society was not adapted to his, of course many alterations would naturally be made. All the log houses still standing in the place, he intended to remove, and only brick and framed edifices should be permitted to remain. Also all enclosures about particular gardens, as well as all the enclosures within the place itself, he would take away, and only allow the public highways leading to the settlement to be enclosed. The whole should bear a resemblance to a part, in which the separate houses should be scattered about.[18]

Owen's experiment attracted many eminent Americans, including a group of scholars and educationalists who came from Pittsburgh on a boat built specially by William Maclure and called the *Boatload of Knowledge*. Another inhabitant of New Harmony was Frances Wright, a Scotswoman who was a friend of Lafayette and who had founded the anti-slavery colony of Nashoba, near Memphis, in 1825.

Important experiments were carried out, particularly in the field of scholastic organization, but the enterprise soon collapsed under the strain of economic difficulties and internal discord. In Owen's absence one of his followers set up a clandestine whisky distillery; Maclure soon founded a rival community, Macluria, and was promptly imitated by others, so that Owen was forced to sell the property in 1828. He then unsuccessfully attempted to expound his parallelogram system to President Jackson and the Mexican general Santa Anna.[19]

It was only then that Owen, back in England once more and considerably impoverished, met the real public for whom his

[18] Bernhard, Duke of Saxe-Weimar-Eisenach, *Travels through North America during the Years 1825 and 1826*, Philadelphia, 1828, Vol. II, p. 108.
[19] At the same time as the New Harmony experiment, other followers of Owen attempted to establish similar societies in Scotland, at Orbison in 1826 and at Ralahine in Ireland in 1831; but these, too, were short-lived.

theories were destined: the working classes and their embryonic trade unions.

In 1824 the combination laws were repealed, and during the following years many workers' associations were formed. The co-operative movement—which was already in existence at the end of the eighteenth century[20] and given new impetus by George Mudie[21]—was actively encouraged by William King, who published the newspaper *The Co-operator* from 1828–30, and by a London group led by William Lovett and Henry Hetherington.[22] On his return from the United States Owen assumed the leadership of the co-operative movement, founded the National Equitable Labour Exchange in 1832 (where the goods produced were to have been bought and sold with labour-notes) and tried to encourage a unified movement for the immediate reform of the English economy and English society. In 1833 the building workers announced the formation of the National Building Guild of Brothers, declaring themselves ready to take over the whole of the building industry on a co-operative basis and offering work to their members in the new organization. Shortly afterwards trade union delegates from all over the country met at the Labour Exchange to create a great national union, which had as many as a million members, but which soon clashed with the government and was disbanded in 1834.

After these events, Owen remained aloof from public affairs, but his influence continued to bear fruit. Many trade unions and co-operative societies seriously discussed his theory of parallelograms, and indeed took steps to put it into practice. There was an Owenite community at Queenswood in Hampshire from 1839–45

[20] The first co-operative mills were founded in Woolwich and Chatham about 1760; the first consumers' co-operatives were set up in Scotland: the Fenwick Weavers' Society in 1769 and the Govan Victualling Society in 1777; a tailors' co-operative was founded in Birmingham in 1777 and the first co-operative store, the Oldham Co-operative Supply, was opened in 1795.

[21] In 1821 Mudie founded the London Co-operative and Economical Society, whose members lived communally, and in 1821–4 he produced the first co-operative periodical, the *Economist*.

[22] It was in connection with these activities that the word 'socialism' was used for the first time, in 1827, by the *Co-operative Magazine*, see B. Russell, *op. cit.*, p. 200.

and more important still, particularly after the collapse of Chartism in 1842, Owen's theory was to have profound influence on the second phase of the co-operative movement, which began with the Rochdale Pioneers.

This society was founded in 1844 by an Owenite group, who hoped that, by starting with a consumers' co-operative, they would gradually develop into a fully-fledged communal organization. This second aim, however, was gradually lost sight of, as the number of single enterprises grew in numbers to include a co-operative mill, weavers' society and a building society.

The year 1848 saw the appearance of the Christian socialists and John Malcolm, who had studied the French experiments of Philippe Buchez, and in 1863 the North of England Co-operative Society was founded. This Society soon spread throughout England and in 1868 to Scotland. Meanwhile in 1852 a law had been passed legalizing co-operatives, and in 1870 a national co-operative union was set up.

Thus during the period of prosperity after 1846, and in the political climate of the new reformist conservatism which grew up after the 1848 Revolution, the Owenite ideal was settling into an exclusively economic mould, which took no account of the political and town-planning implications which Owen had objectively regarded as inseparable from economics.[23]

THE SCHOOL OF SAINT-SIMON

While he was still a boy, the Count of Saint-Simon (1760–1825) saw a carriage coming towards a child playing in the street; any philanthropist of the old school would have rushed to save the child by picking it up from the street, but the future preacher of

---

[23] Owen's model was taken up again by J. M. Morgan, during the eighteen-thirties, when he formulated his plan for a Christian Commonwealth (published in 1850). This new type of community was to be called the Self-Supporting Institution and was to consist of 300 families living in four-room cottages, spread over 1,000 acres. It was Owen's Utopia, but with the addition of religion. One of J. M. Morgan's supporters was J. S. Buckingham, the author of the plan of Victoria which will be discussed later on.

socialism planted himself in front of the on-coming vehicle so that the child could play in peace.

Thus in his own way, and in a manner quite unlike that of the English reformers, he anticipated the scale of values from which the reforming action of French socialism was to spring.

Saint-Simon and Fourier, like Owen, had grown up in the atmosphere before the 1789 Revolution; indeed, Saint-Simon had been personally involved in the early phases of the movement; but within the limits of revolutionary political discussion there was no room for outlining the underlying social problems and their implicit connections with town-planning.

It is for this reason that, in France as in England, the origins of modern town-planning are to be sought in the black years of the post-war period and Restoration, when speculative thought first attempted to bridge the gap between the hopes aroused by the Revolution and the reality of things as they were.

In France, however, this sense of disappointment was political and ideological rather than economic; the most serious consequences of industrialization and of the rush to the towns were not felt until after 1830, while the artificiality of traditional forms of settlement was exposed by the attempt, partial though it was, to put new life into the *ancien régime*.

It was during this time that Saint-Simon formulated his theory of society,[24] based on the principle that the *industriels*, i.e. the technicians and working classes, should occupy the position of power and overthrow the old ruling classes. After his death in 1825 his teaching was carried on by a group of disciples— Rodrigues, Enfantin, Chevalier—who founded the newspaper *Le Producteur* in 1826 and prepared a systematic exposition of their common theory between 1828 and 1830.[25]

After the 1830 Revolution Saint-Simon's followers attained more freedom, they gained control of the *Globe* and gathered in a

[24] C. R. de Rouvroy Saint-Simon, *Du système industriel* (1821); *Catéchisme des industriels* (1823-4); *Nouveau Christianisme* (1825).
[25] *Exposition de la doctrine de Saint-Simon*, Paris, 1828-30.

semi-monastic community, which even wore a special uniform, first in the Rue Monsigny in Paris and later in Ménilmontant.

The leaders of this group, who bore the title of *pères suprêmes*, were Barthélemy Enfantin (1796–1864) and Amand Bazard (1791–1832); but when Enfantin put forward his theory of 'free love' to replace the 'tyranny of matrimony', Bazard withdrew and Enfantin began to stress the political character of the group, until it was dispersed by the police in 1832.

After this Enfantin tried several times to convert King Louis Philippe to his ideas; in 1841 he was made a member of the Scientific Study Commission for Algeria[26] and, in 1845, secretary to the Paris–Lyon Railway Company. He also played a part in the setting up of the Société d'études pour le canal de Suez, after a personal attempt in 1837 at convincing the Viceroy Mehemet Ali of the desirability of the scheme.[27]

Neither Saint-Simon nor his followers turned their attention to town-planning in any sort of technical detail (Chevalier, admittedly, did propose a fantastic plan of Paris in the *Globe* of 1832, according to which the city was to take the form of a man walking) but they did communicate a desire to operate on a large scale and put a moralistic emphasis on the value of public works—the *grands travaux*—which were later to be of great importance.

FOURIER AND HIS INFLUENCE IN EUROPE AND AMERICA

Very different was the teaching of Charles Fourier (1772–1837) who had none of the public-spirited enthusiasm of the Saint-Simonians but who created a meticulously exact Utopia based on a highly complex philosophical and political system.

This he first expounded in a long treatise which was published anonymously in 1808.[28] He believed that a society based on the rivalry of individual or class interests was immoral and absurd, and suggested that what was needed, to reach a state of universal

[26] B. P. Enfantin, *Colonisation de l'Algerie*, Paris, 1834.
[27] Cf. G. Isambert, *Les Idées sociales en France dès 1815 à 1848*, Paris, 1905, pp. 189–91.
[28] *Théorie des quatre mouvements*, Lyon, 1808.

harmony, was a joint effort. This harmony could only be attained by eliminating the restrictions and conflicting interests which limit the satisfaction of human passions in the existing world and by reforming society in such a way as to guarantee the untrammelled satisfaction of individual tendencies while respecting the rights and privileges of others.

Since he did not have to consider the immediate realization of his plans, Fourier continued to discuss his system further and more fully in his successive works.[29]

After the July Revolution he had a wider hearing; he began to attack other socialist schools of thought[30] and, in 1832, to publish a weekly newspaper *Le Phalanstère ou la Réforme Industrielle* which ceased publication in 1834, reappeared again in 1836 as *La Phalange* and in 1843 began to be published as a daily, *La Démocratie Pacifique*, which continued until it was suppressed in 1850.

According to Fourier's theory, universal harmony was to come about gradually, in the course of seven historic periods. At the time of writing, humanity was in a stage of transition between the fourth period (barbarism) and the fifth (civilization). Civilization is characterized by uncontrolled individual ownership, while the following period (guaranteeism) would establish certain limitations. In this way the chaos and anarchy of contemporary towns would be replaced by absolute order.

The following is the description of the organization of a city of the sixth period:

The city will consist of three enclosures: the first containing the 'cité' or main town, the second containing the suburbs and main manufactories, the third for the 'avenues' and extreme outskirts. Each of the three zones shall adopt different measurements for its buildings, none of which shall be constructed without the approval of a committee of experts, who shall supervise the execution of the following restrictive statutes.

The three zones shall be separated by fences, hedges and plantations which must not obstruct the view.

[29] *Traité de l'association domestique-agricole,* Paris, 1822; *Nouveau monde industriel et sociétaire,* Paris, 1829–30.
[30] *Pièges et charlatanisme de deux sectes, St. Simon et Owen,* Paris, 1831.

Each house in the 'cité' must possess as much free space, in the form of courtyards or garden, as that taken up by the building itself; these spaces will be double in the second zone and triple in the third.

Each house shall stand separately and have regular façades on all sides with ornamentation varying from zone to zone, but excluding bare supporting walls. The minimum space between two houses shall be three toises. . . . The enclosures shall consist only of low walls, topped by grilles or palisades for at least two thirds of their height.

The distance between dwellings shall be calculated horizontally, even on sloping ground, and must be equal to at least half the height of the façade abutting onto it, either on any of the sides or the back.

The houses shall have hip-roofs, though they will have lateral pediments, and shall everywhere have gutters and drainpipes carrying the water down to the pavements.

On the side facing the road the height up to the eaves shall not be greater than half the width of the street. The gaps on either side shall be equivalent to at least one eighth of the width of the façade facing on to the road . . . a necessary precaution to prevent the accumulation of the population at a single point.

The view at the end of each road shall be of a country landscape or of a public or private architectural monument; a regular network of streets will be forbidden. Some will be curved and winding, to avoid monotony. At least one eighth of the surface area will be occupied by squares. Half the streets will be planted with trees of various kinds. The minimum width of the streets shall be nine *toises*; to accommodate the pavements, if they are only for pedestrians, they may be reduced to three *toises,* but the other six shall be kept as flower-beds.[31]

In such a city, 'it will be impossible to build small houses' and all accommodation will be communal, implying the concentration of services and therefore of human relationships.

This description is a striking anticipation of nineteenth-century building regulations, and it credits such regulations with a value which was, of course, to be disproved by subsequent experience. It is Fourier's most important contribution to later town-planning, though for him this system of rules was only a transitional element in the progress towards universal harmony, to be realized in the seventh period.

[31] C. Fourier, *Traité de l'association domestique-agricole* in *Oeuvres Complètes,* Paris, 1841, 2nd ed., Vol. IV, pp. 500–2.

Here the problem of patterns of living was radically re-stated, with a rationally constituted and functional unit, the Phalanx, replacing the indeterminate community, and a single building, the Phalanstery, replacing the formless city:[32]

Let us suppose the experiment to be carried out by a sovereign or rich private individual . . . or by a powerful company wishing to avoid growth by trial and error and immediately to organize the Great Harmony, the eighth period in all its fullness. The following are indications of the steps to be taken in such a case.

It is necessary for a company of 1,500–1,600 persons to have a stretch of land comprising a good square league (say a surface of six million square *toises*) . . . the land shall be provided with a fine stream of water, it shall be intersected by hills and adapted to varied cultivation; it should be contiguous with a forest and not far removed from a large city, but sufficiently so to escape intruders.

Assuming that the necessary land is provided free of cost by the sovereign, the necessary capital would amount to about four million francs, to be divided into 400 shares of 10,000 francs each.

The number of inhabitants was established by the theory which 'fixes at 810 the number of distinct characters forming the complete scale or *clavier général* of characters to form the domestic Great Harmony'. To this should be added 192 children and old people, 450 others to be discounted because of illness, absence on journeys or on business, or because they were novices or temperamentally unsuitable, and 168 *complémentaires doublants* to give any necessary assistance to the active members; there would therefore be 1,620 persons altogether. Male and female were to be in the ratio of 21 to 20, and personal incomes to vary from 20,000 to 50,000,000 francs.

The annual profits were to be divided up as follows:

5/12 to manual labour;
4/12 to share capital;
3/12 to talent.

Everyone could benefit from these three types of profit, also

[32] *Ibid.*, pp. 427–68 (also *Selection of works from Fourier,* tr. Julia Franklin, London, 1901, pp. 137–8).

cumulatively. The ruling of the Phalanx also provided for automatic third-class feeding, accommodation and clothing for every poor member, with subsequent payment according to the amount of work done.

The edifice occupied by a Phalanx does not in any way resemble our constructions, whether of the city or country ... the lodgings, plantations and stables of a society conducted on the plan of series of groups, must differ vastly from our villages and country towns, which are intended for families having no social connection, and which act in a perverse manner; in place of that class of little houses which rival each other in filth and ugliness in our little towns, a Phalanx constructs an edifice for itself which is as regular as the ground permits. ... The central part ought to be appropriated to public uses, and contain the dining-halls, halls for finance, libraries, study, etc. In this central position are located the place of worship, the *tour d'ordre*, the telegraph, the post-offices, the chimes for ceremonials, the observatory, the winter court adorned with resinous plants, and situated in the rear of the parade court.

One of the wings ought to combine all the noisy workshops, such as the carpenter's shop, the forge, all hammer work; it ought also to contain all the industrial gatherings of children, who are generally very noisy in industry. ... The other wing ought to contain the caravansary with its ball-rooms and its halls appropriated to intercourse with outsiders, so that these may not encumber the central portion of the palace and embarrass the domestic relations.

Apart from individual apartments, the Phalanstery must contain many public halls or *Seristéres,* where the *passional series* will take place. ... So that the palace shall not have too extensive a façade (300 *toises* for the central block and 150 for the two wings, according to Fourier himself) the body of the central building and of the wings shall be double, with a space of at least 15–20 *toises* between the two parallel blocks, forming three long courtyards crossed every fifty *toises* by raised corridors at the first floor level, glassed in and heated and ventilated in the usual fashion in Harmony. ...

To save masonry and space, and to accelerate relations generally, the Palace will have to gain in height, consisting of at least three storeys and an attic, apart from the ground floor and mezzanine, which will contain the accommodation and communal halls for the children and old people, separated from the street-gallery, which is the most important part of the Phalanstery. .... A Phalanx is really a miniature town but without open streets, exposed to all the inclemencies of nature; all parts of the building can be reached by a wide street-gallery on the first floor (it could not be on the ground floor, because this is taken up at several points by passages for vehicles); at the ends of this 'street' excellently designed corridors, supported on pillars or not as the case may be, heated and ventilated at all times of year, provide protected, warm and elegant communication with all parts of the building and its dependencies.

The street-gallery does not receive light from both sides, because one side of it adjoins the building; throughout the Phalanstery there are two series of rooms, one getting its light from the outside, the other from the street-gallery, which must be as high as the three floors that look on to it. The doors to the apartments on the first, second and third floors open on to the street-gallery, which has stairs leading to the second and third floors. It will be six *toises* wide throughout the central building and four in the wings when the final constructions are built in about thirty years time; but for the moment, since the financial situation is modest, the buildings will be as economical as possible, particularly since in thirty years time they are to be rebuilt on a much larger scale. The street-gallery will therefore be four *toises* in the centre and three in the wings. The buildings will be twelve *toises* wide, divided up as follows:

gallery 18–24 ft.;
room opening on to gallery 20 ft.;
room directly by outer wall 24 ft.;
two outer walls each 4 ft.;

in all 72 ft. i.e. 12 *toises*. Some of the public rooms will be eight *toises* wide, stretching from the gallery to the outer wall. .... The apartments will be placed in a carefully composed and graded order; they will be of 20 differing prices, from 50–1,000, but one thing that must be avoided is continual progression, which would place all the expensive apartments in the centre of the building so that they would decrease in price as one moved towards the wings (Fourier draws up a sample plan of this 'intermingled' distribution).

The attic floor was to house the *Champ celluaire* or hostel for visitors, and the water tanks in case of fire.

Fourier never lost hope of realizing his Utopia. But in France, the only attempt to realize a Phalanstery was a total failure. In

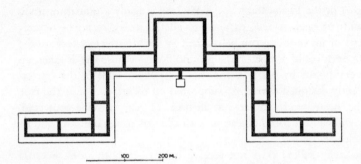

21 Plan of Fourier's Phalanstery, as deduced from the description in the *Traité* and from an engraving produced in the 1841 edition; the *rues intérieures* are shown in heavy black.

1832 M. Baudet Dulary, *député* for Seine-et-Oise, acquired an estate at Condé-sur-Vesgre, near the forest of Rambouillet, to found a Fourierist community, but the capital was inadequate and the enterprise was a failure.

Other attempts were made overseas, in Algeria and New Caledonia and an attempt was made by the Russian philanthropist M. B. Butascevic-Petrascevskij, but his activities were cut short in 1849 by Tsarist reaction. The most fertile ground for Fourier's

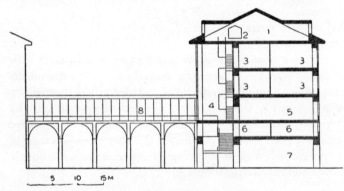

22 Diagram in section of Fourier's Phalanstery, according to the *Traité*: (1) loft with rooms for guests; (2) reservoirs; (3) private apartments; (4) *rue intérieure*; (5) assembly rooms; (6) mezzanine, with accommodation for children; (7) ground floor with space for vehicles; (8) covered footbridge.

62

theories, however, turned out to be America, where they were propagated by Albert Brisbane (1809–90).[33]

Between 1840 and 1850 the movement had considerable success in the United States, where at least 41 experimental communities were founded and where one of Fourier's supporters was Horace Greeley (1811–72), the editor of the New York *Tribune*.[34] The movement also influenced the Transcendentalists of New England, including Charles A. Dana, Parke Godwin and George Ripley, who was the founder of Brook Farm, which was the most interesting of these American experiments.[35]

In the summer of 1841 Ripley and his wife organized an agricultural and educational centre at West Roxbury, Mass. The members of this community (Brook Farm) did manual or intellectual work and enjoyed complete freedom of thought. Their aim was to achieve a harmonious and balanced community, free from the self-interest and rivalry of the contemporary world.

The community worked as a joint-stock company and the profits were divided into a number of portions corresponding to the number of days of manual, or intellectual, work and then distributed among the members according to the number of days they had worked. Each member received one dollar a day, as well as food, lodging, heating and clothing for himself and his family at cost price.

Charles A. Dana and Nathaniel Hawthorne were among the first members, and for the first few years they were in charge of the agricultural activity of the community; other members were John S. Dwight, Minot Pratt, George Partridge, Bradford and Warren Burton.[36] For four years the community also produced a weekly social and political publication, *The Harbinger*.

[33] A Brisbane, *Social Destiny of Man* (1840); *General Introduction to Social Sciences* (1876).
[34] Greeley founded the colony of Sylvania, which lasted from 1842 until 1845; see H. Greeley, *Hints towards Reforms* (1850).
[35] Cf. J. T. Coldman, *Brook Farm*, Boston, 1894; L. Swift, *Brook Farm*, 1900; the experiment is also described in the novel by N. Hawthorne, *The Blithedale Romance*, 1852.
[36] The community was visited by many of the most eminent writers of the time: Ralph W. Emerson, Amos Bronson Alcott, Margaret Fuller, Theodore Parker, Orestes A. Bronson and William Channing.

The enterprise attracted workers of all kinds—carpenters, cobblers, printers—though the majority of its members were always students. The educational complex included a kindergarten, an elementary school and a school with a six-year course for pupils intending to pursue further studies. The students were to devote several hours a day to manual labour, the girls in the kitchen and laundry, the boys in the fields, but they were left free to choose their own course of study.

The community flourished for the first three years of its existence, and four other houses, workshops and dormitories were built around the original farm. At this juncture, because of the growing influence of Fourier's theories, it took on the name of 'Phalanx' and all its financial resources were directed towards the construction of a central building, the Phalanstery. No sooner was this built than it was completely destroyed by fire on the night of March 2nd 1846.

The community did not manage to survive this blow and dispersed in 1849, when the land and building were sold by auction.[37]

The most active of Fourier's followers was Victoire Considérant (1808-93) who went to America after the *coup d'état* of 1851 and, together with Albert Brisbane, visited the North American Phalanx of New Mexico.[38] He too decided to put his theories to the test, purchased some land in Texas and returned to France to publish an appeal (*Au Texas*, 1854) which gained him 250 followers. But the enterprise failed due to lack of capital, and Considérant was left living alone with his family on the farm La Réunion.[39]

[37] On American socialism see M. Hillquit, *History of Socialism in the United States*, 1903; Nordhoff, *Communistic Societies in the United States*, 1875.
[38] This was one of the American Fourierist communities, founded in 1843 by Charles Sears and active until 1854 (cf. C. Sears, *The NAP, a Historical and Descriptive Sketch*, 1886).
[39] Cf. V. P. Considérant, *Exposition du système de Fourier* (1845); *Principes du socialisme* (1847); *Théorie du droit de propriété et du droit au travail* (1848).

One of the people who had helped finance Considérant's attempt had been Jean Baptiste Godin (1817–89), a young industrialist who had started an iron foundry at Guise eight years earlier.

During the Second Empire Godin began to put Fourier's theories of the Phalanstery into practice, modifying them in the light of his own experience. This attempt proved to be the only one that met with any success.

Godin's *Familistère* was a smaller version of Fourier's model: the main premises were still divided into three enclosed blocks, but the small central courtyards round which they stood were glassed over and took the place of Fourier's *rues intérieures*.

The first block was begun in 1859, the central one in 1862 and the third in 1877. Meanwhile, general services had been installed (1860), as well as a crèche and kindergarten in 1862, schools and a theatre (1869) and public baths and a laundry (1870).

In 1880 Godin set up a co-operative and handed the management of the factory and *Familistère* over to his workers. According to Lavedan, the co-operative was still active at the beginning of 1939, the original factory having increased in size.

Godin's theory, presented in his book *Solutions Sociales*,[40] was based on Fourier's co-operative system, and stipulated that profits were to be divided up in accordance with four factors: workers' pay, capital interest, inventors' rights and funds for social security.

But the success of the experiment depended upon two important innovations: the industrial, rather than agricultural, nature of the productive aspect, and the abandoning of the communal life of the Phalanstery, with all the complex consequences foreseen by Fourier. Here each family had its own accommodation, and the *Familistère* safeguarded family autonomy while guaranteeing the advantages of communal amenities.

Here was a striking anticipation of the reasoning on which Le Corbusier's *unité d'habitation* was to be based:

---

[40] Published in Paris in 1870, and known mainly through the translation of M. Howland, which came out in parts in the periodical *Social Solutions* in 1886.

An economic use of land had enabled the *Familistère* to be surrounded by a great park of almost 20 acres. Each apartment has windows looking on to it, both in front, behind and to the sides. . . . Since there is no building facing the *Familistère,* there are no curious neighbours to peer from their windows, whether open or closed. On a fine summer evening each inhabitant has only to close the door opening on to the great hall, to be able to sit at the open window and smoke his pipe or read his book in complete privacy, for all the world as if he were the owner of a separate villa standing in its own grounds.[41]

An elaborate scholastic system catered for the needs of the young from birth onwards:

In the *Familistère* education is organized in seven divisions, each with its own body of directors and teachers, premises and offices. These divisions correspond to the ages of the children:

(*i*) the 'crèche' for children from birth to 26–28 months;
(*ii*) the 'pouponnat' for toddlers to four-year-olds;
(*iii*) the 'bambinat' for children 4–6 years old;
(*iv*) the third class for pupils from 6–8 years old;
(*v*) the second class for children from 8–10;
(*vi*) the first class for children from 10–13;
(*vii*) the 'cours supérieur' for children who, having shown proof of exceptional ability, are to continue their studies;
(*viii*) the 'apprentistat'; in the factory, the boy enters into an apprenticeship free of charge; he is at liberty to choose between the various occupations offered by the *Familistère,* and immediately receives remuneration for his labour.[42]

The first two groups were housed together in a two-storey building, joined to the *Familistère* by a covered passage. The children under the age of two lay in cots, or played, supervised by nurses, in an enclosed space communicating with a covered terrace at the same level; here they learned to walk, using 'a double set of circular railings. This is another co-operative invention. . . . The children crawl and tumble until they reach the

[41] E. Owen Greening, 'The Co-operative Traveller Abroad', in *Social Solutions,* No. 6, 6.8.1886 (this is an account of a visit to Guise; the periodical also publicized the Topolobampo enterprise, in Mexico, mentioned by E. Howards in Chap. IX of *Tomorrow*).
[42] J. B. Godin, 'Social Solutions', in *Social Solutions,* No. 10, 8.9.1886.

23 and 24 *Pages 68 and 69* Plan of the Familistère at Guise (from J. B. Godin, *Solutions Sociales,* 1871).

A. Inner courtyard: (a) thoroughfares on ground floor; (b) steps from cellar to attic; (c) thoroughfares on all floors; (d) gallery; (e) lavatories and waste pipes on all floors (dotted line shows cesspools); (f) hydrants on all floors; (g) chutes for rubbish; (h) rooms with baths and showers; (i) store-rooms and shops for groceries, wines, liqueurs, haberdashery, clothes, shoes, etc.

B. Nursery-school and crèche: (j) nursery-school; (k) rooms for cradles and nurses' beds; (l) the promenade, to help the children learn to walk; (m) office; (n) washing facilities and lavatories for nurses and children; (o) space for gymnastics for two- to four-year-olds; (p) play-room and schoolroom for four-year-olds; (q) outside covered passage, communicating with garden and fields.

C. Schools: (r) entrance corridors; (s) room for general assemblies and theatrical performances; (t) 'bambinat' for children from 4 to 6 years; (u) classroom for third class, children from 6 to 8; (v) classroom for second class, children from 8 to 10; (x) classroom for first class, children of 10 and over; (y) stage; (z) lavatories.

D. Courtyards of surrounding buildings: (a') slaughter house; (b'b') kitchens; (c') restaurant; (d') room for billiards and other games; (e'e'e') coach-houses; (f'f'f') stables, pigstyes, hen-runs; (g'g') bakery; (h'h') cafe, casino (club); (i'i'i') workshops.

E. Laundry, baths and swimming pool: (j') office; (k'k') laundry; (l'l'l') basins for washing; (m') bowls for rinsing; (o') bathrooms; (p') private baths; (q') indoor swimming pool.

F. Gasometer.

F

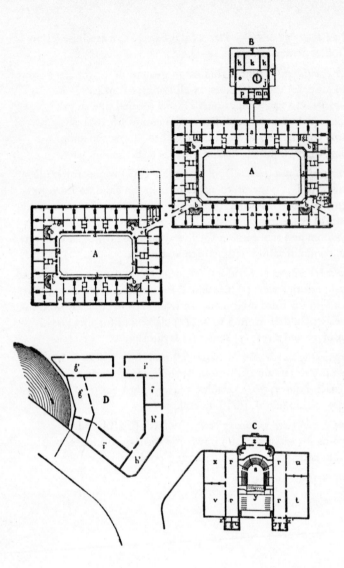

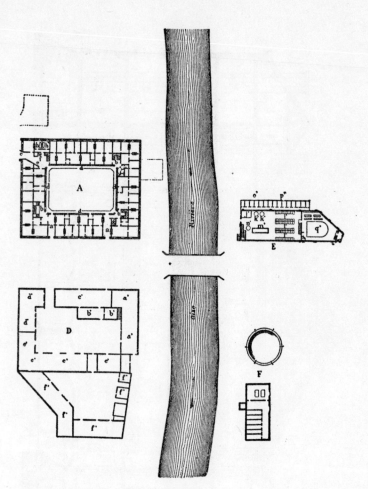

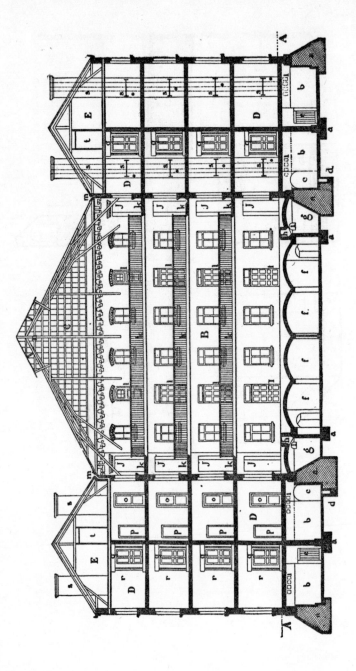

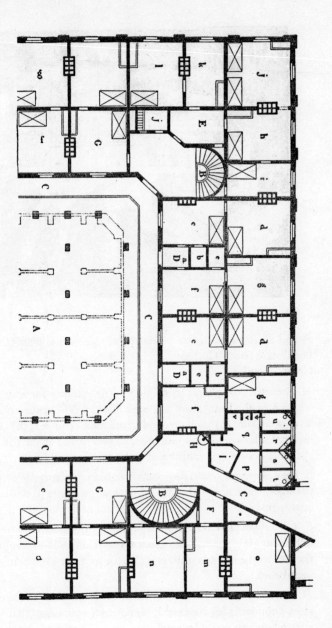

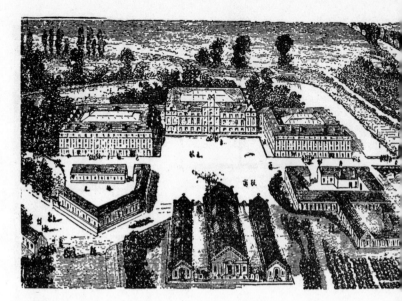

25 and 26 *Pages 70 and 71* Transverse section and plan of the
Familistère (from Godin).
Godin's captions:

A. Basement: (b) cellars; (c) corridors; (d) entrance for water-pipes
which feed the four floors and tank in attic; (e) outside entrance, on
level of façade; (g) underground ventilation chamber; (h) openings of
underground ventilation chamber; (i) ventilation shafts for
apartments between vaulting of cellar and ground-floor.

B. Inner courtyard, ground floor and upper floors: (j) entrance to galleries,
passages, stairs and hydrants; (k) general galleries; (l) doors to
apartments.

C. Glass roofing over courtyard and galleries: (m) waste-pipes (for rain
falling on glass roofing and inner hollows of roof) passing through
the loft to the outside gutters; (n) hip-roof over glass roofing for
ventilation.

D. Interior of apartments: (o) entrance from corridor; (p) larder and
store cupboard; (q) cupboard; (r) door set in wall, so that two
apartments can easily be made into one if required; (s) air shaft in
chimney for ventilation of each apartment.

E. Loft: (t) corridors.

72

27 View of the Familistère (from Godin). On the left are the three
residential blocks, surrounded by the curve of the river; in front are
the workshops and the building which houses the schools and
theatre. On the right are the factories and the first house of the town
of Guise.

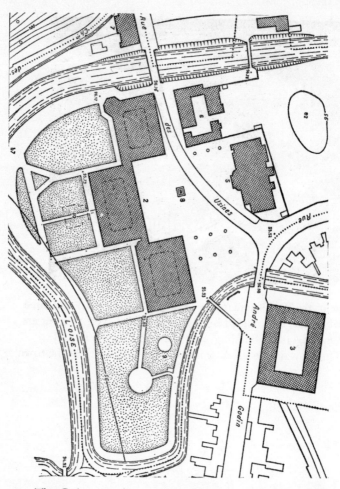

28   The Guise complex as it is today (from Auzelle): (2) the
Familistère; (3) building with new accommodation built after 1886;
(5) schools and theatre; (6) workshops; (7) laundry and baths.

railing, then they pull themselves to their feet and begin to walk around in a circle, holding on to the bars'; in the adjoining section children from two to four learned 'to talk correctly, to count, sing and dance, to form lines and squares, by means of pleasant games, and to understand the pictures on the walls.'[43]

The schools for children from four to thirteen years of age were in another two-storied building facing the *Familistère* and between the two symmetrical schoolrooms stood the theatre, which was also used as an assembly hall for meetings and student performances.

Figures 23, 24 and 25 bear Godin's original captions and additional information. In 1886 the community consisted of about 400 families, and was certainly the most successful of the many attempted by socialist theoreticians during the nineteenth century.[44]

THE EGALITARIAN TRADITION AND CABET

The 1830 and 1848 uprisings were haunted by the memory of the French Revolution, for it was this that had moulded the feelings and experiences of the entire French nation. One of the most frequently remembered episodes of the Revolution was the Babeuf conspiracy, and it was brought back to the public's attention in 1828 when Filippo Buonarroti published his *Conspiration pour l'égalité, dite de Babeuf*.

In this conspiracy, which took place in 1796, political action was justified by the theoretical vision of a future egalitarian society briefly described in the conspiratorial documents and more fully described by Buonarroti after the event. In the following passages he discusses the rational use of land:

Since the inequality of fortunes has condemned one portion of the people to overwhelming toil, and another portion to a demoralizing

---

[43] J. B. Godin, *loc. cit.*, No. 5, 16.7.1886.
[44] But even this was judged negatively by the Marxists, in the *Socialiste*, Paris, 1886; cf. Engels, *The Housing Question* (1872), London, 1942.

inaction; the country parts have comparatively few inhabitants, often insufficient for the wants of cultivation, but always crushed under the weight of excessive fatigue. The supernumerary population has crowded into cities, either to dissipate there in voluptuousness the riches produced by the country people, or to procure an easy living by subserving the pleasures of the rich, or through the complications of the public administration.

In verging towards equality, society should necessarily witness the breaking up of those huge gatherings of human beings, which are destructive alike of morals and population. Those capable of work should necessarily return to the country to lighten the burden of their rustic brethren. The industry of towns would go to embellish the lives of the country people who feed them. The simplicity of the new government would render unnecessary the myriads of clerks and placemen who are now abstracted from agriculture and the useful arts; and the maintenance of order being dependent on the due discharge by each citizen of his respective functions, it would no longer be compatible with those tumultuous gatherings in towns, amongst which it is so easy to hide one's actions from public observance and censure.

No longer a capital—no more great cities—the country would be gradually but rapidly covered with villages, built in the most healthy and convenient places, and located in such a manner as to communicate easily with one another, by means of roads and numerous canals, which it would be in every respect in the general interest to open and construct.

It is to be presumed, that all considerations yielding to the supreme law of equality, the sumptuous mansion and towering castle would give place to the salubrity, commodiousness and prosperity of all the habitations, disposed with an elegant symmetry, both to please the eye and facilitate the maintenance of public order.

As there would no longer be palaces, neither would there be any miserable ruins, such as now constitute the greater number of habitations. The dwellings would be simple, and the magnificence of architecture and the arts, which set off and heighten its imposing grandeur, would be reserved for the public magazines, for the amphitheatres, for the circuses, aquaducts, bridges, canals, public places, the archives, libraries and, above all, for the places consecrated to the deliberations of the magistrates, and to the exercise of the popular sovereignty.[45]

[45] F. Buonarroti, *History of Babeuf's Conspiracy* (1828), tr. Bronterre, 1836, p. 160.

Together with Saint-Simon and Fourier, Buonarroti is the third important source of French Utopian thought after 1830 and, according to Jules Prudhommeaux, he was a direct source of inspiration for Etienne Cabet (1788–1856).

Cabet played an active part in the 1830 Revolution and was appointed Attorney-General of Corsica, but he soon antagonized the Orleanist government and was exiled to England, where he met Owen. Here he wrote a Utopian novel, *Voyage en Icarie*, which was published in 1840, when he was able to return to France after the amnesty of 1839.[46]

The novel, possibly inspired by Thomas More's *Utopia*, describes an imaginary country, Icaria, and its capital Icara, which is a great metropolis divided into two by a straight stretch of river and built on a completely geometrical plan, with neatly intersecting roads ringed by two circular boulevards.

The collective organization of the economy has made retail trade, and therefore all shops, superfluous and these are replaced by state stores and *atéliers*. Cemeteries, workshops of all kinds and hospitals are situated outside the city in the countryside. Traffic is controlled for the safety of pedestrians, who use special covered passages, while vehicles run only on special tracks and must keep to the right.

The city is made up of sixty districts, each of which 'bears the name of one of the great nations'. All the houses in a single street are identical and are modelled on 'the most pleasant examples of the houses of foreign countries'.[47]

Cabet put forward his political programme—total communism, to be achieved by persuasion and not by violence—in the periodical *Le Populaire*, and he soon had a considerable following. In May 1847, encouraged by his success, he published the manifesto called *Allons en Icarie* and, at the same time, a pamphlet

---

[46] Cabet's theories are alluded to in his historical works *Histoire de la révolution de 1830* (1831); *Histoire de la révolution française* (1840); and more fully in his *Le Vrai Christianisme de Jésus Christ* (1846).
[47] Quoted in P. Lavedan, *Histoire de l'urbanisme, époque contemporaine*, Paris, 1952, p. 86.

called *Réalisation de la Communauté d'Icarie* in which he announced that he could count on 10,000 to 20,000 men to put his plans into action.

In December Cabet announced that he had chosen a site in Texas, where the Peters Company, as the concessionaire of government land, was to make available 'over a million acres'.[48] On 3rd February 1848 an advance group of sixty-nine persons embarked at Le Havre, but several days later the revolution broke out and most of his followers gave up the idea of leaving. Cabet himself was involved in the early phases of the revolution and was an unsuccessful candidate in the April elections for the Constituent Assembly.

Meanwhile, the advance party had arrived at their destination, where they learned that the land consisted of a number of separate lots of 320 acres each; and so, after unsuccessfully trying to settle on several of these, they moved to New Orleans, where they were joined by 400 more companions during the same year. Cabet filled his company with new courage when he joined them in December and obtained a new site in Illinois, where he purchased the village and small-holding of Nauvoo, on the banks of the Missouri, from Brigham Young and his Mormons.

The Icarians arrived in Nauvoo in March 1849, where they built their town making use of the buildings and ruins left there by the Mormons, but illness and defection soon reduced their numbers to 260. They organized a refectory for communal meals, a school, library and theatre which was much frequented by the inhabitants of the surrounding countryside. Families lived in separate apartments, and bachelors in double rooms.[49]

[48] It is probable that Cabet contacted the Peters' Company through Owen, who had made a similar attempt in 1828. A fully documented account of the Icarian colonies in the U.S. is given in J. Prudhommeaux, *Histoire de la communauté icarienne*, Nîmes, 1906.
[49] Here is a description of the main buildings of Nauvoo. The school: 'the most notable building in the colony was the school, built entirely of freestone, the debris of the Mormon temple. From a distance, it looked as though it were made of white marble. Divided into two sections, it held 30–40 boys and as many girls. The classroom, which was fairly spacious, and the large dormitories struck me at once with their spotless cleanliness. Two wide courtyards, shaded by acacias, provided the

But economic difficulties and internal disputes continued to jeopardize the community's existence. In 1856 a real schism developed when Cabet and a small number of the faithful moved to St. Louis where Cabet died in the November of the same year. His followers settled in the suburbs of Cheltenham, but their numbers declined to twenty, and in 1864 they dispersed.

The majority who had stayed in Nauvoo decided to sell their common possessions and in 1860 they emigrated to Corning in Iowa, where they at last found a suitable site for their activities in the form of a 3,000-acre estate. Here the thirty-five remaining Icarians realized their ideal city and in fact achieved a certain prosperity and when the French traveller M. A. Massoulard visited Icaria in 1875 the number of inhabitants had risen to seventy-five. The arrangement of the houses is reminiscent of Owen's parallelogram:

Icaria is situated almost at the centre of the estate. The Icarians call their dwellings collectively 'the city' (ville); in the centre is the refectory, set in the middle of a huge square. Three sides of this square are occupied by detached houses, the gaps between them being filled by decorative gardens. The fourth side is devoted to common amenities, the laundry, bakery etc.

children with space to pass their leisure hours playing games in the open air. They took pause from mental effort by growing flowers in small enclosures, and also enjoyed gymnastics. In this way both boys and girls made the acquaintance of manual tasks. The boys gathered wood for the heating system, distributed water and transported victuals. The girls did the washing up, prepared the fruit and vegetables, folded the printed pages (for the printing works). There was also, for the girls, a tailors' workshop where they made the clothes for the elderly members of the community.' (Holynski, in *Revue Socialiste,* Sept. 1892, p. 296, quoted in J. Prudhommeaux, *op. cit.,* p. 133.)

The printing works: 'Our printing office produces works in French, German and English. We have produced three newspapers in these three languages, many pamphlets, manifestoes etc. for the internal administration. The Icarian printing office is also at the service of outsiders and earns sums of considerable importance.' ('Report on the Situation in 1855', published in *Colonie Icarienne,* p. 159; Prudhommeaux, *op. cit.,* p. 109.)

The refectory: 'There are 12 doors and 12 windows. Normally one enters through the door facing the open space, and through the other doors when necessary. There are two doors into the kitchen, and through one of them the plates are carried on a sort of long railway. Bread is placed on, and in, a long sideboard, while the fountain of drinking water is placed on another smaller one.' ('Report' *cit.,* pp. 111–12; Prudhommeaux, *op. cit.,* p. 109.)

The situation is pleasant, being on a hill which slopes as meadow-land down to a stream, on which the mill also stands, about half a mile distant; the other slope of the hill is thickly wooded and will shortly be transformed into a splendid garden. The farm stands on another hill, about a quarter of a mile away. And about a quarter of a mile beyond that lie the ploughed fields.

Icaria is a most delightful looking place. The great building of the refectory, surrounded by a clustering semi-circle of small houses, backs on to a great dark wood which emphasises the little white-painted houses. Fruit-trees and exotic flowers and trees, and meadows, separate the various parts of the village. Unfortunately there is no water, and this is a serious inconvenience because it necessitates a transport service which uses a man and cart for half a day; it also involves economy, possibly too great, in the use of water.

Accommodation usually consists of two rooms, one a living room and the other a bedroom. On the top floor, in the attic, are two small rooms for the children.[50]

But in 1879 this idyll was shattered by yet another schism; the farm split into two and a party of socialist leanings, the 'young party', was left in possession of the village. Soon afterwards, however, this group, numbering only twenty people, moved to California where it founded Icaria-Speranza, which remained in existence until 1887.

The other party settled about a mile from the original village and founded New Icaria, where it obstinately tried to recreate the harmonious atmosphere aimed at from the beginning:

The plans of the new building were drawn up in the summer of 1879. The heads of the community, acting as extempore architects, designed the building for general accommodation, and various lesser ones, to stand on either side of the building housing the main hall . . . in September 1879 the first house, on wooden rollers, was placed in its appointed position in the square. Others followed and so, finally, did the hall itself, which was to be the centre of community life. Thanks to the unremitting labours of parents and children, the weeds and undergrowth disappeared, to be replaced by groves, meadows, orchards, pleasant flower gardens. Trellises grew, promising shelter from the summer sun; rustic benches tempted the passer-by to rest

[50] J. Prudhommeaux, *op. cit.*, p. 292.

29 Communal building in the Rappite village of Economy (from
C. Tunnard, *The City of Man*).

awhile; the children had a swing, a cricket pitch. In short, within two
years, the clearing was transformed into a park which attracted people
from all the surrounding districts.[51]

New Icaria continued a modest existence until 1895 when the
company disbanded, sharing out its assets between the twenty-
one remaining members.

Cabet's ambitions, in fact, underwent a sort of *reductio ad
absurdum*, and the idea of a great metropolis led to the formation

[51] From descriptions given by survivors, quoted in J. Prudhommeaux, *op. cit.*,
pp. 390–1. The relationship between Owen and Cabet, and the Protestant sects of
America suggest a certain similarity between socialistic and religious communities
that has not previously been elaborated. The 'Harmonists' founded by the German
George Rapp, settled in Pennsylvania, in Indiana (where they sold Owen the village
of Harmony in 1825) and then at Economy, nr. Pittsburgh. Other communities
founded by German reformers were Amana, Zoar, Bethel and Aurora. In 1842 the
Perfectionists, led by John H. Noyes, built Oneida, in the state of New York (cf.
J. H. Noyes, *History of American Socialism*, Philadelphia, 1870). The Norwegian
violinist Ole B. Bull settled in America in 1852 and founded Oleona, New Norway,
New Bergen and Valhalla (cf. M. Smith, *The Life of Ole Bull*, Princeton, 1943). The
cities founded by the Mormons were particularly important: Nauvoo in 1839
(subsequently handed over to Cabet) and Salt Lake City in 1847.

of ever smaller country villages which finally dwindled to the size of normal private units.

This tale of the difficulties and defeats encountered by the promoters of nineteenth-century Utopias suggests an immense amount of wasted energy and their practical failures seem to confirm the harsh theoretical judgement passed on them by Marxist writers.

The Communist Party Manifesto of 1848 contains the following passage:

The founders of these systems see, indeed, the class antagonisms, as well as the action of the decomposing elements in the prevailing form of society. But the proletariat, as yet in its infancy, offers to them the spectacle of a class without any historical initiative or any independent political movement.

Since the development of class antagonism keeps even pace with the development of industry, the economic situation, as they find it, does not as yet offer to them the material conditions for the emancipation of the proletariat. They therefore search after a new social science, after new social laws, that are to create these conditions.

Historical action is to yield to their personal inventive action, historically created conditions of emancipation to fantastic ones, and the gradual, spontaneous class organization of the proletariat to an organization of society specially contrived by these inventors. Future history resolves itself, in their eyes, into the propaganda and the practical carrying out of their social plans. . . .

Hence, they reject all political, and especially all revolutionary, action; they wish to attain their ends by peaceful means, and endeavour, by small experiments, necessarily doomed to failure, and by the force of example, to pave the way for the new social Gospel.

Such fantastic pictures of a future society, painted at a time when the proletariat is still in a very underdeveloped state and has but a fantastic conception of its own position correspond with the first instinctive yearnings of that class for a general reconstruction of society.

But these Socialist and Communist publications contain also a critical element. They attack every principle of existing society. Hence they are full of the most valuable materials for the enlightenment of the working class. The practical measures proposed in them—such as the abolition between town and country, of the family, of the carrying on of industries for the account of private individuals, and of the wage system, the proclamation of social harmony, the conversion of the functions of the State into a mere superintendence of production, all these proposals point solely to the disappearance of class antagonisms which were, at that time, only just cropping up and which, in these publications, are recognized in their earliest indistinct and undefined forms only. These proposals, therefore, are of a purely Utopian character.[52]

Yet time has shown that this judgement should be amended. The 'first instinctive yearnings' of those who inspired and carried out these experiments did in some ways go beyond the classical Marxist scheme, and anticipated the present-day need to consider political and economic problems independently, rather than jointly and as part of a single programmatic formula.

The suggested solutions for the problem of modern town-planning must necessarily be abstract and schematic, since any realistic assessment of the links between the process of town-planning and the general development of social and economic relations is entirely lacking. This tends to foster the illusion that the functioning of society in general and of town-planning in particular are identical, and that the second can be dealt with at the same rate, and with the same methods, as the first.

But Marx and Engels, basing their observations on a direct analysis of economic relations, implicitly accepted this identity by inverting the two terms and assuming that changes in town-planning were a necessary consequence of altered social relations: hence their indifference to the problems of town-planning and the vagueness of their arrangements for the form of future communities.[53]

In this context the Utopians' tendency to intervene immediately, without waiting for any general reform of society, can be seen as a really valuable source of inspiration and their ideal cities

[52] K. Marx and F. Engels, *Manifesto of the Communist Party,* Foreign Languages Publishing House, Moscow, 1955, pp. 112–14.
[53] 'To want to solve the housing question while at the same time desiring to maintain the modern big cities is an absurdity. The modern big cities, however, will be abolished only by the abolition of the capitalist mode of production ...' cf. F. Engels, *The Housing Question* (1872), p. 50.

take their place in the history of modern town-planning as models of generosity and sympathy, quite different from the ideal cities of the Renaissance.

The theoretical descriptions given by Owen, Fourier and Cabet also contributed largely to that great store of ideas by which later town-planning experiments, up to those of the present day, were inspired. There is an obvious and impressive similarity between certain of their proposals—the *unité d'habitation* with a limited number of inhabitants, centralized services and specially equipped courtyards, the *rue intérieure* with traffic circulating on ground level—and certain developments of modern architecture. Even the number of inhabitants proposed by Owen for his parallelogram (1,200) and by Fourier for his Phalanstery (1,620) is roughly that suggested by Le Corbusier for his *unité d'habitation*, and Owen's suggested population density, one inhabitant per acre, is that suggested by Wright for Broadacre City.

The theoretical research carried out by Socialist reformers was to be drawn on by Ebenezer Howard for his Garden Cities and by the post-war German planners of the *Siedlungen,* though here the concept of the ideal city was diluted and it was made merely an expendable limb of the modern metropolis; a more or less independent satellite quarter. But the pre-1848 designs and experiments have a lasting claim to our consideration in that they aimed at something far more ambitious: at the total reconstruction of the urban and rural landscape in accordance with the emergent social and economic problems.

2 the beginnings of town-planning legislation in England and France

During the years of the Industrial Revolution the majority of the roads, bridges, canals and ports throughout the country had been constructed by private enterprise and the State, unless it had strategic reasons for intervening, preferred to restrict its intervention to a general and vague surveillance, exercised through the formalities of authorization and patent.

In Britain the building and upkeep of the original roads had been the responsibility of the parish, by means of *corvées* imposed upon local inhabitants. The inefficiency of parish administration, which became increasingly marked throughout the course of the eighteenth century, allowed roads to decline just when traffic was increasing. It was to remedy this situation that the 1745 Parliament began to promulgate the Turnpike Acts, allowing private individuals to build new turnpikes. At the same time the technical contributions of Telford and Macadam made possible unparalleled improvements in quality and durability, so that the old regulations limiting the weights and sizes of vehicles on the principle of adapting the traffic to the roads, could be repealed.

The remaining difficulties were connected with the petty particularism of the numerous trusts managing short stretches of road, and the continued existence of a huge network of country roads administered by the parishes. In 1820 the State was forced to intervene in order to establish some degree of consistency in the running of the toll roads, and again in 1835 to abolish the *corvées*, empowering local authorities to levy a rate for the upkeep of the roads. Toll-roads were gradually abolished between 1858 and 1895, and the expense of the upkeep of the roads was assumed by the various counties in 1888.[54]

The network of English canals was built by individual mine-owners and groups of speculators following the example of the Duke of Bridgewater, who opened the first commercial canal, near Manchester, in 1761. Between 1890 and 1894 canal-building mania caused a positive boom in speculation. The State authorized the individual enterprises but stipulated that the canals should be open to anyone wishing to use them upon payment of a tax.[55]

But the invention of a new means of transport, the railway, changed things completely. The first railways were used experimentally near mines, and towards the beginning of the nineteenth century public transport trunk lines opened, though the carriages were still horse-drawn. The first experimental steam trains proved to be more expensive than the horse-drawn ones[56] until the invention of Stephenson's locomotive, which ran the first public service between Stockton and Darlington, in 1825. The first important line, from Manchester to Birmingham, was opened in 1830, and it was then that this new method of transport began to compete with the traditional means. At first an attempt was made to apply the type of ruling governing the use of roads and canals, which prescribed that the tracks should be open to any user on payment of the designated toll, but this soon proved impossible,

[54] Cf. E. L. Bogart, *Economic History of Europe, 1760–1939*, London, 1942, p. 145.
[55] *Ibid.*, pp. 146–8.
[56] A first model was built in France by G. Cugnot, in 1769; after Watt's invention several other attempts were made by Robinson and Murdock between 1780–90, and by Trevithick in 1803.

since the various buildings firms all insisted on managing their own lines. Parliament was not long able to uphold its traditional criterion of non-intervention and trust in free enterprise to ensure the efficient working of the services. Thus in 1844 it passed a law providing for the optional State purchase of the railways within 21 years (though at the expiration of this period, in 1865, the altered political circumstances made it advisable to retain a privately-run system) and laid down regulations for the speed, timing and tariffs to be maintained on the existing lines.

Similarly, in the early stages of construction, as long as the stretches of line remained separate, the builders could use different gauges; but when the various trunk-lines were joined together to form a single network, the State had to intervene and, in 1846, fixed a standard gauge of four feet eight and a half inches.[57]

In France the *ancien régime* had left the country a good road system, maintained by *corvées* of local inhabitants. This system was abolished by the Revolution and the State assumed direct responsibility for building and maintaining the roads. Napoleon I built many roads of strategic importance in France and the occupied countries, rejecting the expedient of toll-roads; the Restoration government did much to improve secondary roads and, in 1818, drew up a plan for the building of canals, to be undertaken by private companies who were authorized to levy tolls and the July Monarchy, which set up a Ministry of Public Works in 1831, put forward an immense programme for the building of roads and canals, to which it allocated about 800 million francs during the following decade.

The problem of railway building was immediately tackled in a most far-sighted fashion. The first railway, near St. Etienne, opened in 1832, and as early as 1833 the government directed the Conseil général des ponts et chaussées to outline a plan for the whole country; but the proposal that the State should be responsible for building the railways, as in Belgium, was repeatedly rejected (in

[57] E. L. Bogart, *op. cit.*, pp. 150 ff.

1835, 1837 and 1838) and for some time the authorities proceeded piecemeal, granting concessions to individual private companies. The increasingly urgent need for some centralized control, however, led to the law of 1842, which gave large private companies the monopoly of the main lines, dividing expense almost equally between State and private capital, and stipulating that the railways were to become State property at the end of forty years.[58]

The new programmes of public works, especially those for the railways, made it practicable for public administration to make really basic modifications in the utilization of land, and in the shape of the towns—striking examples are the 1842 railway plan for France, with seven lines converging on Paris, and the consequences of the fact that the position chosen for railway stations was generally at the edge of a town. But such was the urgency and complexity of technical demands that the overall planning potential of these new developments passed almost unnoticed and both legislation and practice acquired a specialized, departmentalized character, so that relations and connections between the various sectors were lost from sight.

This was therefore unpromising terrain for the growth of town-planning legislation, and indeed the specialized legislation on railways and public works was later to prove one of its most powerful obstacles.

The only important consequence of these developments, as far as town-planning was concerned, was the revision of the laws of compulsory land acquisition. This had previously been regarded as something both rare and exceptional but now, since it was being applied on a large scale, it was regulated to the ever increasing advantage of the State.

In England in 1840 the measures taken to protect the rights of landowners made the cost of building the railways five times

---

[58] *Ibid.*, p. 155 ff. As early as 1837 F. Bartholomy, president of the Compagnie d'Orléans, declared that: 'the application of steam can only be compared, in its importance, to the invention of printing and the discovery of America, events which have changed the face of the earth' (quoted in H. Peyret, *Histoire des chemins de fer en France et dans le monde*, Paris, 1949).

higher than in the German states and ten times higher than in America, where railways were spreading into the empty expanses of the west.[59] In England too the procedure for land acquisition was formally regulated between 1842 and 1845.

In France the Napoleonic law of 1810 and the Orléanist law of 1833—necessitated by the programmes of public works discussed above—were perfected in 1841, just before the national plan for the railways, by the law of 13 May, which was to serve as a model for the laws of many other countries, including the Italian law of 1865. This law established that the acquisition of land must be authorized by the legislature, that it must be defined in detail by prefectorial decree and ordered in individual cases by the judiciary, which would also settle any controversies that might arise.

But the basic pattern of planning problems created by the Industrial Revolution emerged, naturally enough, when people began to be really affected by the sanitary conditions brought about by the disorder and overcrowding of the new suburbs. It was only when these became intolerable, with the cholera epidemics which were widespread after 1830, and when the first measures to eliminate them were studied, that it became apparent that there was not one, but a whole number of basic causes, and that preventive measures would have to be various, yet co-ordinated. In this way sanitary legislation was the direct forerunner of modern town-planning legislation, and it soon diffused the idea of compulsory land acquisition by extending its use from public works to include the whole body of a town.

In England the first serious attempts to improve sanitary conditions in the towns were carried out after the Reform Bill of 1832, and they formed an integral part of the new Whig programme of reform.

In the same year, 1832, Edwin Chadwick (1800–90), a former assistant of Bentham's, was appointed Inspector of the Poor Law Commission; he helped to formulate the new law of 1834 and

[59] Quoted by A. P. Usher, *An Introduction to the Industrial History of England*, London, 1939, p. 449.

was the leader of all reform in the field of public health until his retirement from public life in 1854.

In many ways, the 1834 Poor Law Amendment reflected the theoretical prejudices, radical in origin, characteristic of the ruling classes then in power.

The disastrous Speenhamland system was abolished, thus establishing the principle that no one should receive partial subsidies; workhouses were provided for the unemployed, but always with the proviso that they should 'make life more unpleasant for their inmates than that of the most miserable of independent labourers'.[60] At the same time a far more efficient system of supervision was organized, with a central authority and local 'Unions' for each group of parishes. These were also responsible for the medical care of the poor and therefore for the register of births and deaths—the latter classified according to cause, in accordance with the Registration Act of 1836—and also, after 1840, for public vaccination.

Chadwick, who was appointed secretary to the central commission, was able to find out a great deal about the living conditions of the poorer classes, but he also realized that the powers hitherto granted by law to these Unions permitted them to take action that was, at most, palliative; the causes of the disastrous sanitary situation were linked inseparably with the kind of buildings in which people had lived and were living, and with the fact that traditional methods of intervention were no longer efficacious.

There were in fact numerous public commissions in the cities (300 in London alone) which were supposed to be responsible for lighting, street-paving, drainage and water-supplies, or for the enforcement of building, traffic and police regulations, but they were discredited and incapable of adapting themselves to the technical difficulties caused by the rapid development of the new towns. In 1835 new elective municipal administrations were set up to take over the tasks previously performed by these various

[60] These are the words of Nassau Senior, who, together with Chadwick, was responsible for the law; the workhouses, of course, were described by Dickens in *Oliver Twist* (1838).

traditional bodies, but they had not yet been granted the powers necessary for effective action, while corresponding curtailments of the rights of the private individual had still to be introduced.

Because of the importance of private enterprise in English legislation and customs, this innovation proved lengthy and difficult, and it was only the dramatic testimony of the cholera epidemics, which occurred repeatedly from 1831 onwards, that persuaded the authorities to emerge from their traditional stronghold of non-intervention.

In 1838 the London authorities asked the Poor Law Commission to make enquiries about the origins of an epidemic in Whitechapel.

The report of the Commission—which consisted of three doctors, Arnott, Kay and Southwood Smith—and especially Southwood Smith's personal report on the lack of water, made a profound impression on public opinion. In 1839 Chadwick gained permission from Lord Russell to extend the enquiry to the whole country; he compiled the final report in 1842, which for the first time provided a complete picture of the sanitary conditions of the working classes.[61]

Meanwhile, a House of Commons committee had taken up the matter and had published a report confirming Chadwick's conclusions in 1840 and soon afterwards Peel, encouraged by Lord Ashley and the Prince Consort, appointed a Royal Commission on the State of Large Towns and Populous Districts, which published its findings in 1844 and 1845.[62]

Perhaps the most interesting feature about the proposals put forward by the Royal Commission for improving hygiene in towns, was their variety. They included suggestions for:

—delegating responsibility for sanitary control to local authorities, under the direct supervision of the Crown;

[61] 'Report on the Sanitary Conditions of the Labouring Population', 1842; cf. J. H. Clapham, *An Economic History of Modern Britain, the Early Railway Age,* Cambridge, 1939, Ch. I.
[62] 'First Report of the Commissioners for Inquiring into the State of Large Towns and Populous Districts', 1844; 'Second report etc.', 1845.

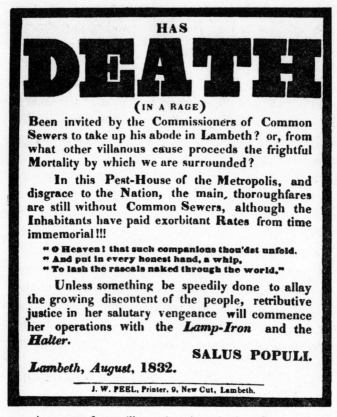

HAS

DEATH

(IN A RAGE)

Been invited by the Commissioners of Common Sewers to take up his abode in Lambeth? or, from what other villanous cause proceeds the frightful Mortality by which we are surrounded?

In this Pest-House of the Metropolis, and disgrace to the Nation, the main, thoroughfares are still without Common Sewers, although the Inhabitants have paid exorbitant Rates from time immemorial!!!

" O Heaven! that such companions thou'dst unfold,
" And put in every honest hand, a whip,
" To lash the rascals naked through the world."

Unless something be speedily done to allay the growing discontent of the people, retributive justice in her salutary vengeance will commence her operations with the *Lamp-Iron* and the *Halter.*

SALUS POPULI.

Lambeth, August, 1832.

J. W. PEEL, Printer, 9, New Cut, Lambeth.

30 A poster of 1832 illustrating the agitation about sanitary conditions in London (from L. Wright, *Clean and Decent*).

—preparing surveys and detailed investigations of a district before planning the drainage system;

—co-ordinating work on sewerage with work on the roads;

—allocating funds to local authorities for road widening and improvement;

—laying down minimum sanitary requirements for all dwellings and making efficient sanitation obligatory;

—giving the authority power to insist on adequate ventilation and compulsory cleansing of foul houses, and to introduce the use of a licence for lodging-houses;

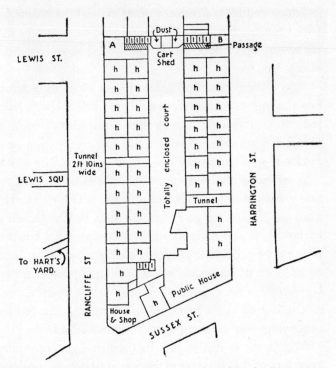

31 Plan of a courtyard in Nottingham; reproduced in the *Report on State of Large Towns and Populous Districts*, 1845 (from Hoskins).

—setting up a regular panel of medical officers of health;

—granting funds for the opening of public parks in industrial cities which had none.

It was already obvious that future sanitary legislation would have to develop within the general framework of town-planning legislation, and that, once one problem had been isolated for consideration—that of sanitation—all others would necessarily follow.

The first legal consequence of these reports was the law of 9 August 1844 for London and the surrounding district,[63] which laid down certain minimum sanitary requirements for rented

[63] 7 & 8 *Victoriae Reginae*, C. lxxxiv; 'An Act for Regulating the Construction and the Use of Buildings in the Metropolis and its Neighbourhood', p. 190.

lodgings and forbade the use of cellars and basements for human habitation as from July 1846. During the same year the first law for the setting up of public baths and wash-houses in the capital was also passed.

Also during 1846 Parliament began to study a more general law dealing with the same problems; and while politicians and journalists dwelt at length upon liberalism's time-honoured theoretical arguments against public intervention, a new cholera epidemic spoke eloquently in favour of immediate action.

A bill based on the recommendations of the Royal Commission was presented in 1847 but subsequently withdrawn and it was not until the following year that the first Public Health Act was approved. It was more limited than the original but nonetheless of immense political importance, as it represented, at least in some of its more striking aspects, the first attempt to adapt traditional legislation to the realities of the new urban situation.

The law of 31 August 1848 is a long and detailed document, occupying over seventy pages of the official acts.[64]

The length is due in part to English legal convention but in part, too, to the character of the new law; it was introducing a new concept of public control into a field not previously regulated, or regulated by contradictory and antiquated precepts, so that its relationship with other current laws required a long and detailed series of definitions. The definitions of the terms used, in fact take up almost three pages.

The objects of this law are expressed as follows: 'whereas further and more effectual provision ought to be made for Improving the sanitary condition of Towns and populous places in England and Wales, and it is expedient that the Supply of Water to such Towns and Places, and the Sewerage, Drainage, cleansing and paving thereof be placed under one and the same Management and Control, subject to such general Supervision as is herein after provided . . .' (art. 1).

[64] Statutes at Large, vol. 88, c. 63, art. I. 11 & 12 *Victoriae Reginae*, 'An Act for Promoting the Public Health'.

The first thing the law did was to set up the General Board of Health, consisting of three members appointed by the sovereign, one secretary and the necessary staff. The General Board of Health could appoint inspectors to conduct local enquiries if requested by at least one-tenth of the inhabitants, or if the death rate had been over twenty-three per thousand over the last seven years (arts. 3–8).

Following such enquiries the General Board of Health would encourage the application of the new law, by setting up special 'districts', which might or might not coincide with the ordinary administrative ones (subject in some cases to approval by local assemblies) (arts. 9–11).

Each district was to have a local Board of Health, consisting of special staff and representatives of landlords and rate-payers. The following articles (12–33) deal with the methods of electing these representatives.

The Board of Health could appoint inspectors, clerks and also a doctor who might then become Officer of Health (art. 40). Local Boards were empowered to deal with:

(a) sewerage (arts. 41–54); most important of all, the law states that the local Board shall 'cause to be prepared a Map exhibiting a System of Sewerage for effectually draining their district, upon a scale to be prescribed by the Board of Health'.

Furthermore, 'all sewers, whether existing at the time when this Act is applied or made at any time thereafter (with certain exceptions) together with all Buildings, Works, Materials and Things belonging or appertaining thereto, shall . . . be entered under the Management and control of the Local Board of Health'. The compulsory purchase of the relevant possessions of the previous owners is also provided for. Each newly-built house must have its own drains and lavatory; anyone contravening this clause would have to pay a fine of up to £20, and the local Board might order the lavatory to be built at the owner's expense. Owners of new buildings also had to declare the level of their cellars or lowest floor, and the exact situation of the lavatories and cess-pools,

32 Main drainage in Paris (corner of Rue Soufflot and Rue St. Jacques; from A. Joanne, *Paris Illustre,* 1870).

which must be approved by the local Board; anyone not complying could be fined up to £15 and forced to carry out the relevant alterations and improvements.

(*b*) Refuse collection (arts. 55–57).

(*c*) The removal of anything likely to cause danger to health (open drains, pigsties, rubbish heaps, stagnant water in cellars etc. (arts. 58–60).

(*d*) Inspection of slaughter houses (arts. 61–65).

(*e*) Inspection of lodging houses (arts. 66–67) which must have a certain standard of cleanliness and ventilation. The use of cellars as dwelling rooms, unless they fulfilled certain conditions, was prohibited, and all occupied cellars not fulfilling these regulations were to be evacuated within a period of six months to a year.

(f) The paving and upkeep of roads (arts. 68–73).

(g) Public gardens (art. 74): 'the local Boards of Health, with the approval of the said General Board, may provide, maintain and improve premises for the Purpose of being used as public Walks or Pleasure Grounds and support or contribute towards any Premises provided for such purposes by any Person whomsoever.'

(h) the water supply (arts. 75–80).

(i) the burial of the dead (arts. 81–3).

Article 117 also states that these local Boards were to be responsible for the supervision of the State roads.

The following articles (84 onwards) are concerned with the administration and financial workings of the local Boards, and they state that the expenses incurred by the installation of the various services may be recuperated in two ways: by the payment of special district rates, to be paid by owners of property benefitting from these installations, and by 'general district rates' applicable to the whole district. When the work carried out is for the improvement of private property, its owner was to pay special 'private improvement rates'.

The relationship between Board and individual was minutely regulated by the last articles. Landlords had many legal safeguards, but it was inevitable that the exercise of the full rights of ownership should be curtailed in various ways by the new law. Quite apart from having to observe the regulations, pay the rates and possibly even have his property requisitioned, the private owner had to guarantee Board of Health officials free access to his property at all times, 'to draw up plans, inspect, measure, level, supervise work in progress, examine the course of sewers and drains, inspect or fix boundaries'.

The law did not apply to the City of London (which had its own very powerful Commissioners of Sewers), to the districts served by the Commission of Sewers set up on 13 November and 4 December 1847, or to the Regent's Park area, which had been under special supervision since 1825.

The debate accompanying the bill's passage through Parliament is extremely interesting because of the variety and insistence of the objections put forward, not only by the property-owners and their representatives, who were personally involved, but also by liberal theoreticians such as Herbert Spencer.[65] The episode is quoted by Walter Lippmann as a typical example of the kind of distortion that could be produced by the policy of non-intervention.

The radical *Economist*, 13 May 1848, expressed regret that the Public Health Act had not met with the opposition it deserved, and scornfully refused to go into details of the matter, since the law dealt with 'a great variety of matters which we cannot even enumerate, without crowding our space with a catalogue of somewhat offensive words' (sewers, refuse heaps, etc.). It went on to observe that 'suffering and evil are nature's admonitions; they cannot be got rid of; and the impatient attempts of benevolence to banish them from the world of legislation before benevolence has learned their object and end, have always been productive of more evil than good.[66]

All Chadwick and his colleagues could set against these philosophical arguments was common sense and the undeniable reality of the epidemics rife in London at this time. But the specialists' alarm was fully justified for this law constituted the first step in the direction of a vital change in procedure, a change which was not going to remain within the bounds set by the legislators of 1848.

The local Boards began to function slowly and laboriously. During the first phase of the law's application a decisive part was played by the General Board of Health (composed of two eminent politicians, Lord Shaftesbury and Lord Morpeth and two sanitary experts, Chadwick and Southwood Smith) which functioned for ten years amid continual controversy until its abolition in 1858, when its work was carried on by the private Council. In this

[65] H. Spencer, *Social Statics* (1851); cf. W. Lippmann, *The Good Society*, London, 1938, p. 298.
[66] J. H. Clapham, *op. cit.*, p. 545; cf. B. Russell, *Freedom and Organization, 1814-1914*, London, 1934, p. 133.

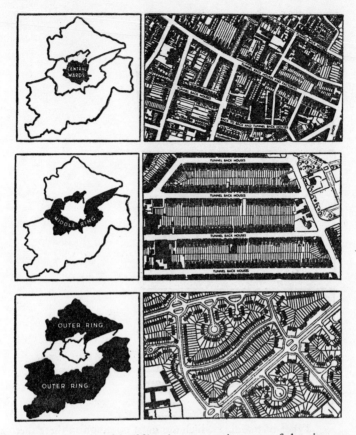

33   Birmingham, regulated building in concentric zones of the city, illustrating the development of building regulations from the middle to the end of the nineteenth century (from F. Hiorns, *Town Building in History*).

period it managed to set up 183 local Boards and to gain approval, in 1851, for the first law on subsidized housing, which was later modified in 1868 and 1875. But now the course of English sanitary legislation could not be changed; the next steps were the setting up of the Local Government Board (with jurisdiction over both the health and welfare of the poor) and the new sanitary law of 1875, until finally the laws concerning subsidized housing and

99

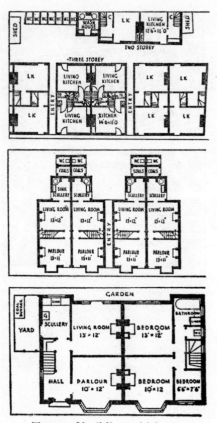

34 Types of building which are most common in these three zones: three storey houses with outdoor WCs, two storey houses with WCs attached, semi-detached houses with gardens.

health were amalgamated by the Housing of the Working Classes Act of 1890.

In France the consequences of industrialization and of the movement to the towns were not felt until later, but from 1840 onwards sanitary conditions in the big cities and industrial centres were just as alarming as in England.

In 1840 Frégier, an employee of the Prefecture of the Seine, drew up a plan of public buildings for the poorer classes[67] and in

[67] *Des classes dangereuses de la population dans les grandes villes et des moyens de les rendre meilleures,* Paris, 1840.

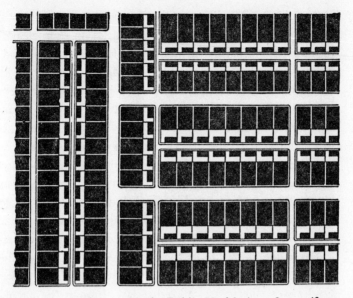

35 Housing in accordance with the Public Health Act of 1875 (from
C. Bauer, *Modern Housing*). The rulings of the earliest building
regulations on height, detachment etc., interpreted to the letter by
builders so as to obtain the maximum density permissible, made the
building in the new suburbs uniform and dreary. During the burst of
speculation which produced the first jerry buildings, these regulations,
though respected, were not really efficacious; it was plainly necessary
to vary the regulations from place to place and to issue them within
the framework of an overall plan.

the same year Villermé produced the first documented enquiry
into the conditions of the life of labourers.[68] But throughout the
July monarchy the unchallenged rule of the liberal *bourgeoisie* made
it impossible to take any effective measures limiting private
building and private ownership and so the battle against insanitary housing was carried on by the two main opposition
parties: the Catholics and the Socialists.

In 1842 the Society of St. Vincent de Paul set up a commission
to study the sanitary conditions of workers' dwellings in Lille.

[68] L. R. Villermé, *Tableau de l'état physique et moral des ouvriers*, Paris, 1840.

In 1845 the Société d'Economie Charitable began to publish the *Annales de la Charité*, where various articles on slum clearance in working-class districts appeared.[69] The leading spirit behind these activities was the Count Armand de Melun, later active in promoting the first town-planning law during the Second Republic.

The Socialists were working towards the same ends, and the heartfelt descriptions in the *Annales de la Charité* were echoed in Blanqui's report on the French working classes in 1848.[70] But the Socialists viewed the problem more in terms of their own theories, imagining that a new economic organization would completely solve both the housing problem and all other social ills. It was for this reason that the Catholics, who tended to take problems one by one, were the more active promoters of town-planning reform.

During the short life of the Second Republic the studies and proposals which had been worked out during the two previous decades were finally crystallized as law through the agencies of Armand de Melun and his brother Anatole, who presented a bill to the National Assembly in 1849.

Melun's bill was considered first by a parliamentary committee headed by M. de Labordère, then by a committee of members of the Assembly headed by M. de Riancey. In the official report M. de Riancey, anticipating the inevitable attack from the opposition, presented the new law cautiously but firmly: 'the matter is a delicate one ... the free use, the free availability of the citizen's possessions demands the strictest respect, since it constitutes the basis of all social order.' Nonetheless, in numerous cases 'the rights and interests of private individuals must yield before the interest of the public', and various restrictions concerning the right of ownership were already in existence: it was prohibited to sell bad foodstuffs, or to put a ship to sea in poor repair. These prohibitions did not undermine the principle of ownership, on the contrary they protected it: 'Nothing better

[69] Mme. de Craon, *Du logement du pauvre et de l'ouvrier*, 1845, pp. 393–402; H. Romain, *Des classes ouvrières*, 1847, pp. 747–62.
[70] J. A. Blanqui, *Des classes ouvrières en France pendant l'année 1848*, Paris, 1849.

justifies ownership than the very authority of the law, which regulates and sanctions it.'[71]

The law was attacked both by the Thiers liberals, defenders of the 'rights of man', and by the Socialists, already disappointed by the failure of the *ateliers nationaux* and distrustful of any partial measures for reform.

Among the more significant protests was an article in the *Revue des deux monds* by a former Saint-Simonian, Michel Chevalier,[72] and another in the socialist paper *La Voix du Peuple,* which prognosticated darkly about the fate of working-class families driven from insanitary slums, unable to find better accommodation they could afford and therefore reduced to 'seeking another refuge as yet undiscovered by the police, or to sleeping in the open'.[73]

Various highly significant amendments were proposed and rejected during this debate: one for example, put forward by Roussel, suggested extending the measures for slum clearance to include whole districts, and one by Wolowski suggested authorizing the Commune to build new houses in the place of the old ones that were to be demolished.

A last cholera epidemic in 1849 was probably the deciding factor, and the law was passed on 13 April 1850. More limited in content than the English law, it simply laid down regulations for lodging houses and put the enforcement of the law into the hands of Commune officials, without making provisions for any central and co-ordinating body.

Article 1 stated: 'In all communes where it is deemed necessary by the Municipal Council, a Commission shall be appointed to investigate and outline the measures vital to the improvement of slum dwellings and their dependencies, either rented or occupied by people other than the owners, the tenant or user.' Article 2

[71] Quoted in J. Hugueney, *Un Centenaire oublié: la premiere loi d'urbanisme, 13 avril 1850* in *La Vie urbaine,* 1950, p. 246. The report is reproduced in *Annales de la Charité,* 1849, pp. 725–36.
[72] 15.3.1850, p. 976.
[73] 7.3.1850; cf. the reply of M. de Melun in the parliamentary proceedings reported in the *Moniteur.*

defined the nature of the Commission, which was to include an architect and a doctor, not necessarily resident in the Commune. The subsequent articles distinguish the various causes of insanitary conditions; if the owner is responsible, then he must carry out the work needed to eliminate them, on penalty of fines which could amount to twice the total cost of the necessary improvements. Finally, Article 13 stated that 'when this unwholesomeness is the result of external and permanent causes, and when these causes cannot be removed without basic alterations, the Commune, following the forms and procedure set down by the law of 3 April 1841, may acquire the sum total of the property included within the limits of the relevant works'.[74]

The whole importance of the law lies in this article. Unlike England, France already had efficient legislation for compulsory acquisition, based on the law of 1841.

This law, devised for public works, could now be applied to the clearance of residential quarters and it was the same law that enabled Haussmann to realize his radical transformation of Paris during the following two decades, when he profited from an amendment of 23 May 1852, which gave the executive the power to acquire land without having recourse to the courts.

[74] J. Hugueney, *op. cit.*, p. 246.

1848 and its consequences

Just as the 1848 Revolution was the turning point in the history of nineteenth-century culture and political achievement, so it was a crucial moment in the history of modern town-planning.

A systematic study of the relationship between politics and town-planning does not yet exist, and thus hints and hypotheses, which can be confirmed only by further research, must be the basis for any discussion of the subject. But even the little documentation that there is is sufficient to reveal the vital importance of the 1848 crisis in this field as in all others.

The long period of common struggle against the Orleanist régime in France had brought about a certain degree of *rapprochement* between the working-class and *bourgeois* opposition movements, and it was this that made possible the amalgamation of the Republicans of Ledru-Rollin and Cavaignac with Blanc's Socialists in 1843.

The motive for this temporary union was not purely strategic: the weight of the whole of the working class, by now conscious of its plight and anxious to better it, lay behind these political groups.

Their aim, expressed in elementary terms by those directly concerned ('in this way you will obtain your just and legitimate deserts'—wrote the labourer Efrahem—'i.e. wages sufficient to feed you, your wives and your children')[1] took on overtones of urgency and immediacy, while managing superficially to reconcile the contradictory aims of the various factions. There was no time for delay or discussion: 'Parliament is too slow for the people' observed John Fielden in 1833.[2]

Practical experience of the temporary government which had emerged from the February Revolution soon shattered any agreement between the various parties which had come to power, and the great hopes that had produced it. According to Marx's classic interpretation, the events of the spring of 1848 revealed the perennial reality of class warfare existing behind the false front of common aims, of a basic enmity which set the *bourgeois* parties against the socialists; they also exposed the absurdity of the idealism of the socialists, who hoped to realize their organizational aims without clarifying the conflict of interests that existed between the forces involved, and without adopting a positive line of action with regard to hostile elements.

After stating that it would guarantee all citizens the right to work, the provisional government set up the *ateliers nationaux* on 27 February. This was one of Blanc's basic ideas, but it was put into practice by the Republican Minister Marie in such a way that it was bound to be a failure. Blanc had proposed genuine State intervention in industry, with workers employed in those sectors for which they were best suited and in accordance with a comprehensive vision of economic development, while the hundred thousand workers organized by Marie were digging pointlessly in the Champ de Mars. But the totally unprofitable employment of the workers of the *ateliers nationaux* was merely symptomatic of the widespread failure in 1848 to translate a political revolution successfully into a series of carefully calculated interventions in

---

[1] Quoted in E. Dolléans, *Histoire du mouvement ouvrier,* 3rd ed., Paris, 1947, p. 49.
[2] *Op. cit.,* p. 109.

time and space. In this context the slogans on the banners of the Parisian demonstrators of 28 February—'Ministry of Progress', 'Organization of Labour'—can be seen not only as references to various points of Blanc's programme but also as allusions, still purely emblematic, to the development of economic and urban planning, which was gradually to fill the ideological void of the time.

Proudhon, with the sensitivity of the anti-conformist, observed as early as 26 February: 'So many words and not a single idea! . . . the government, having no ideas, does nothing, wants to do nothing. How easily they drift towards dictatorship!'[3]

The workers' revolt of June 1848, after the closure of the *ateliers nationaux*, made the socialist-propounded economic revolution impossible once and for all and the working-class movement emerged from it shattered and confused, though conscious at last of the conflict of interests fermenting beneath the political dispute, and of the need to tackle it on a higher analytical and organizational level; the movement entered a new phase which was scientific and international.

The Manifesto of Marx and Engels, written a month before the events in France, was the main text for this new dispute, which led up to the first International in 1864. The stress was now on the central political problem of ownership and power, which was considered prejudicial to any change in working-class conditions; every partial reform, realized within the framework of the capitalist system, would develop into a confirmation of this system and must be regarded as completely invalid.

In his inaugural address of 1864 Marx repeated and enlarged on the criticisms of reforming and Utopian Socialism which he had already made in the Manifesto. The matter was taken up again during the first meetings of the International, between Marx and Bakunin, primarily as criticism of the current experiments, and it was one of the causes which led up to the dissolution of the association in 1873.

[3] *Op. cit.*, p. 230.

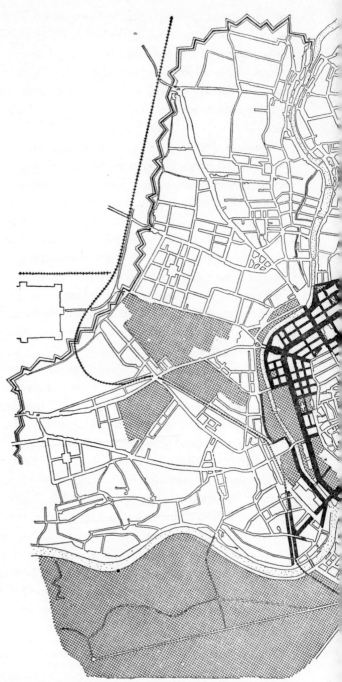

36 Vienna, the network of roads around the old city built between
1859 and 1872 in the region of the old fortifications.

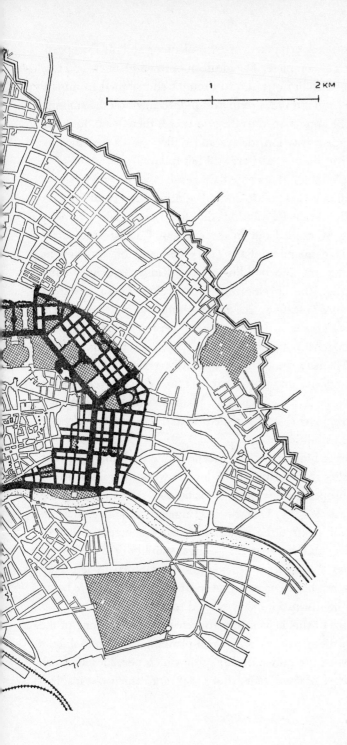

Now the rift between practical town-planning and the European political left was complete. The idealism of town-planners and the increasing inflexibility of political thought contributed to this in equal degree, and if there is room for disagreement on the amount of blame to be apportioned to the two causes there is no doubt at all that the disorientation, delays and difficulties caused by this rift were felt in the past and are still felt today.

In town-planning, the immediate result was to encourage a purely technical viewpoint; indeed, during the twenty years following the 1848 Revolution the first large-scale planning operations were carried out in the cities of Europe—the *grands travaux* of Haussmann in Paris (1853–69), and of Anspach in Brussels (1867–71), the building of the Ringstrasse in Vienna (1857 onwards), the development of Barcelona (1859 onwards) and of Florence (1864–77), the re-designing and installation of a main drainage system in London where, between 1848 and 1865, Joseph Bazalgette completed the new system of main sewers along the Thames, the Victoria and Albert Embankment, and where the Underground was begun in 1863. These developments were the work of a new class of planners and civil servants, scientific, competent, and satisfied with their various departmental responsibilities.

But however independent this technical activity might appear to be, in reality town-planning fell largely within the influence of the new European conservatism. Napoleon III in France, the young Tories led by Disraeli in England and Bismarck in Germany soon realized the importance that a coherent policy of public works could have on the political stability of their respective countries. Partial reforms, even those proposed by left-wing oppositions, might be effected to prevent too much pressure being exerted on the institutions they wished to preserve.

The origins of this new ardour for reform, of which one of the most conspicuous aspects was town-planning, are undoubtedly bound up with the humanitarian spirit which pervades so much of the literature of the decade before 1848, and which was inspired partly by the spirit of the Socialist Utopias. But it was more usually inclined to replace clear-cut decisions by a vague feeling of compassion for the sufferings of the poor which expressed itself in an equally vague appeal for universal solidarity.

In contrast to the black pictures of the hovels of the industrial city painted by Kingsley, Elizabeth Gaskell, Dickens and Sue, and side by side with the idealized descriptions of the good old days, when there was no industry, one does sometimes come across a description of what living and working conditions could be like in a modern industrial community, if only social relationships were based on good will, rather than on economic antagonism.

The figures who have the authors' sympathy are the many philanthropists and enlightened industrialists, like the Cheerybee brothers in *Nicholas Nickleby* (1839) and the M. Hardy who appears in Sue's *Le Juif errant* (1845). The following is the description of the model village built for his workers by M. Hardy:

M. Hardy's factory that morning looked as gay as the bright sky above it.

Side by side with the industrial building used exclusively for manufacturing purposes, there stood another large building divided into so many smaller apartments, where the workers lived. On the ground floor were a number of co-operative shops selling a variety of goods, a laundry, an evening school, a first aid centre and recreation rooms of all sorts, all organized and managed by a central administration of factory employees. The whole had been studied and organized by M. Hardy (who had supplied the necessary capital) with such providence and wisdom that rents and foodstuffs cost almost a third of the normal prices, and furthermore payments could be made monthly, in that each worker had a sort of current account to which his wages were credited, while rent and other commitments were deducted. And all this could be done without depriving the capital, provided by M. Hardy for this sort of communal dwelling, of a reasonable interest of about 5 per cent. These and many other social measures put M. Hardy's workers in a very privileged position compared with the great mass of other workers, and were the origin of the hatred and envy harboured and fomented against them by interested agitators.

Here are obvious reminiscences of the Utopias of Owen and

Fourier, or rather of their framework stripped of the political implications.[4] But it would be absurd to scrutinize Sue's straightforward description for a hint of ideological recantation, least of all for any betrayal of his socialist convictions.

Disraeli, however, discusses the same subject in his contemporary novels with very precise political implications.

Coningsby, the protagonist of the novel of the same name (1844), goes to Manchester and takes careful note of the industrial world he finds there; he is an aristocrat who, nevertheless is not in the least unnerved by the new reality of industry:

It was to him a new world, pregnant with new ideas, and suggestive of new trains of thought and feeling. In this unprecedented partnership between capital and science, working on a spot which nature had indicated as the fitting theatre of their exploits, he beheld a great source

[4] E. Sue, *Le Juif errant* (1845), part XIV. In another novel, *Les Misères des enfants trouvés*, of 1851, there is another description, politically more explicit and containing obvious reminiscences of Fourier's Phalanstery: 'The castle of Conte Duriveau had undergone a complete transformation. The main body of the building, with its two lateral wings, was still standing, and these two wings had been lengthened so as to form an immense parallelogram, joined by new buildings so as to run parallel to the original main building and form a complete whole. A wide stone portico, running along the inside of this parallelogram, formed a terrace on the first floor, while the ground floor included a covered passage which enabled people to circulate within the great construction without fearing either sun or rain. The ground enclosed was cultivated as a garden. Its avenues and paths led to a circular central point, with a crystal clear fountain. This monument, of stone and wrought iron, was topped by a spherical ornament which bore the following words in large letters: "None has a right to the superfluous until each has the necessary." In the evenings the garden, the building and the portico were illuminated by gas, whose light was reflected here and there in the park, and on to a wood of ancient trees that had been conserved and that stretched away behind the castle. Lastly, to the right of this parallelogram, from amid the numerous buildings which had been added externally, rose the immense chimneys of the various steam engines serving either to facilitate certain tasks, or to draw and circulate the water which is to be found throughout this immense establishment.'

Then follows a description of the castle's interior: 'Its immense halls had been transformed into schools for the children, and into kindergartens for the infants of the association. One huge room opening on to the winter garden (which had been conserved) acted as assembly hall and refectory for those members of the association preferring to have communal meals rather than transport the food, which was prepared in the communal kitchen, back to their own apartments. The upper floors housed the linen cupboards, infirmary, store-rooms for raw materials of all sorts, of which there were vast quantities, and the huge workshops, because the association was both agricultural and industrial; so that the long evenings and stormy winter days when work in the fields would not have been possible, were profitably utilized.

of the wealth of nations which had been reserved for these times, and he perceived that this wealth was rapidly developing classes whose power was very imperfectly recognised in the constitutional scheme, and whose duties in the social system seemed altogether omitted.[5]

Mr. Millbank embodies the new conception of the type of social relationships that could derive from industry; Coningsby visits his factory the next day:

In a green valley of Lancaster, contiguous to that district of factories on which we have already touched, a clear and powerful stream flows through a broad meadow land. Upon its margin, adorned, rather than shadowed, by some very old elm trees, for they are too distant to serve except for ornament, rises a vast deep red brick pile which, though formal and monotonous in its general character, is not without a certain beauty of proportion and an artist-like finish in its occasional masonry. The front which is of great extent, and covered with many tiers of small windows, is flanked by two projecting wings in the same style, which form a large court, completed by a dwarf wall crowned with a light and rather elegant building; in the centre, the principle entrance, a lofty portal of bold and beautiful design, surmounted by a statue of Commerce.

This building, not without a certain degree of dignity, is what is

[5] B. Disraeli, *Coningsby,* London, 1911, p. 130.

Accommodation consisted, according to the needs of the family, of one or two rooms, all looking on to the inner garden, well-ventilated in summer and well-heated in winter by means of steam. . . . Innumerable conduits piped water and gas for lighting, to all parts of the building. Children and bachelors slept in special dormitories under the surveillance of 'house' mothers and fathers, who were elected for this particular task by turns. The cooking, washing and other skilled or family tasks were performed in specially equipped premises. The associates' private accommodation was for privacy, relaxation and repose only.'

The concern was managed by a co-operative of 763 workers and was founded by the Count Duriveau, a conscience-stricken capitalist who had renounced his rights as landlord and capitalist and now received a share in the company equal to that of the other associates. But in this case too Sue observes: 'this association is not only an admirable institution from a moral point of view, but would also have been an excellent proposition for its founder from a business point of view had he not, out of noble disinterest, renounced all the income he might honestly have claimed from his part in the association. Indeed, two neighbouring landowners, amazed at the results we have obtained, have set up with their tenants and journeymen an association for an agricultural manufacturing enterprise . . . with these rich landowners providing the capital for the initial expense: thus not only are they doing good actions on an immense scale, but they are also increasing their revenues at the same time.'

technically and not very felicitously called a mill . . . and which really was the principal factory of Oswald Millbank. . . . At some little distance, and rather withdrawn from the principal stream, were two other smaller structures of the same style. About a quarter of a mile further on, appeared a village of not inconsiderable size, and remarkable from the neatness and even picturesque character of its architecture, and the gay gardens that surrounded it. On a sunny knoll in the background rose a church in the best style of Christian architecture, and near it was a clerical residence and a school-house of similar design. The village too could boast of another public building; an institute where there was a library and a lecture-room; and a reading hall which anyone might frequent at certain hours, and under reasonable regulations.

On the other side of the principal factory, but more remote, about half a mile indeed up the valley, surrounded by beautiful meadows and built on an agreeable elevation was the mansion of the mill-owner; apparently a commodious and not inconsiderable dwelling-house, built in what is called a villa style, with a variety of gardens and conservatories. The atmosphere of this somewhat striking settlement was not disturbed and polluted by the dark vapour, which to the shame of Manchester still infests that great town, for Mr. Millbank, who liked nothing so much as an invention, unless it was an experiment, took care to consume his own smoke.[6]

Coningsby visits Millbank, listens to his plans for building (the workers' houses are to have a 'new system of ventilation') and learns his political convictions; Millbank does not believe in equality ('I am not a leveller, and I consider artificial equality to be as dangerous as fictitious aristocracy') but he criticizes the nobility of his time, forgetful of its functions and duties, in the name of a 'natural aristocracy' formed of men 'eminent for virtue, talents, and property, and if you please, birth and standing in the land', and capable of 'guiding opinion; and therefore of governing'.[7]

In Disraeli's next novel, *Sybil* or *The Two Nations* (1845) the enlightened industrialist is Mr. Trafford; the account of his life and the description of his factory and model village form part of a coherent, and unambiguously didactic, whole:

[6] *Op. cit.,* pp. 133-4.
[7] *Op. cit.,* p. 142.

A few days after his morning walk with Sybil, it was agreed that Egremont should visit Mr. Trafford's factory. . . . The factory was about a mile distant from their cottage, which belonged indeed to Mr. Trafford, and had been built by him. He was the younger son of a family that had for centuries been planted in the land but who, not satisfied with the factitious consideration with which society compensates the junior members of a territorial house for their entailed poverty, had availed himself of some opportunities that offered themselves, and had devoted his energies to those new sources of wealth that were unknown to his ancestors. His operations at first had been extremely limited, like his fortunes; but with a small capital, though his profits were not considerable, he at least gained experience. With gentle blood in his veins, and old English feelings, he imbibed, at an early period of his career, a correct conception of the relations which should subsist between the employer and the employed. He felt that between them should be other ties than the payment and the receipt of wages.

A distant and childless relative, who made him a visit, pleased with his energy and enterprise, and touched by the development of his social views, left him a considerable sum, at a moment too when a great opening was offered to manufacturing capital and skill. Trafford, schooled in rigid fortunes, and formed by struggle, if not by adversity, was ripe for the occasion, and equal to it. He became very opulent, and he lost no time in carrying into life and being the very plans which he had brooded over in the years when his good thoughts were limited to dreams. On the banks of his native Mowe he had built a factory which was now one of the marvels of the district; one might almost say, of the country: a single room, spreading over nearly two acres, and holding more than two thousand work-people. The roof of groined arches, lighted by ventilating domes at the height of eighteen feet, was supported by hollow cast-iron columns, through which the drainage of the roof was effected. The height of the ordinary rooms in which the work-people in manufactories are engaged is not more than from nine to eleven feet; and these are built in storeys, the heat and effluvia of the lower rooms communicated to those above, and the difficulty of ventilation insurmountable. At Mr. Trafford's, by an ingenious process, not unlike what is practised in the House of Commons, the ventilation was also carried on from below, so that the whole building was kept at a steady temperature, and little susceptible to atmospheric pressure. The physical advantages of thus carrying on the whole work in one chamber are great: in the improved health of the people, the security against dangerous accidents for women and youth, and the reduced fatigue resulting from not having to ascend and descend and carry materials to the higher rooms. But the moral advantages resulting from superior inspection and general observation are not less important: the child works under the eye of the parent, the parent under that of the superior workman; the inspector or employer at a glance can behold all.

When the work-people of Mr. Trafford left his factory they were not forgotten. Deeply had he pondered on the influence of the employer on the health and content of his work-people. He knew well that the domestic virtues are dependent on the existence of a home, and one of his first efforts had been to build a village where every family might be well lodged. Although he was the principal proprietor, and proud of that character, he nevertheless encouraged his workmen to purchase the fee; there were some who had saved sufficient money to effect this; proud of their house and their little garden, and of the horticultural society, where its produce permitted them to be annual competitors. In every street there was a well; behind the factory were the public baths; the schools were under the direction of a perpetual curate of the church, which Mr. Trafford, though a Roman Catholic, had raised and endowed. In the midst of this village, surrounded by beautiful gardens, which gave an impulse to the horti- culture of the community, was the house of Trafford himself, who comprehended his position too well to withdraw himself with vulgar exclusiveness from his real dependents, but recognized the baronial principle reviving in a new form, and adapted to the softer manners and more ingenious circumstances of the times. . . .

The vast form of the spreading factory, the roofs and gardens of the village, the Tudor chimneys of the house of Trafford, the spire of the Gothic church, with the sparkling river and sylvan background, came rather suddenly upon the sight of Egremont. . . .[8]

The first experiments in popular housing, subsidized either by private contractors or by the State, took place in this ideological climate and may, indeed, have been influenced by the ideas put forward by Disraeli between 1844 and 1845.

In 1845 the first Society for Improving the Dwellings of the Labouring Classes was set up, financed by wealthy private indivi-

[8] B. Disraeli, *Sybil* or *The Two Nations* (1845), London, 1937, pp. 183-6.

Modelli d'abitazioni economiche (*disegno di S. A. R. il Principe Alberto*).

37   Workers' dwellings built for the Universal Exhibition of 1851 in London.

duals who renounced all return on invested capital to keep the rents low. In 1846 the Richardsons began to build a village for their workers in Bessbrook, Ireland. During the Universal Exhibition of 1851 a block of model houses was built in Hyde Park, under the auspices of Prince Albert and in the same year the first two laws on subsidized housing were passed, the Labouring Classes Lodging Houses Act and the Common Lodging Houses Act, proposed by Anthony Ashley Cooper, Lord Shaftesbury (1801–84) who had been a member of the Young England group with Disraeli. In 1853 Titus Salt embarked on the building of Saltaire—a model village putting Disraeli's literary descriptions into reality and which, according to Stewart[9] was indeed inspired by the reading of *Sybil*—and during the same year the village of Bromborough was founded for the workers in the Price candle factory. Lastly, an original contribution was made to the improve-

[9] C. Stewart, *A Prospect of Cities*, London, 1952, p. 153. Ch. VIII has a full description of Saltaire, with a bibliography on p. 167.

ment of workers' lodgings by Montague W. Lowry-Corry, who was Disraeli's private secretary from 1866 until the latter's death, and who retired from active politics in 1880, with the title of Lord Rowton. He devoted the last part of his life to a study of the problems of workers' housing and designed a type of building (in which each occupant had a separate cubicle for sleeping) which was first built at Vauxhall in 1892 and was so successful that it led to the founding of a company, Rowton Houses Ltd.

The political interpretation of these enterprises is clear. The Chartist movement, after its show of strength in 1842, gradually began to lose ground, partly because of the mistakes made by O'Connor[10] and partly because of the wave of prosperity which had followed the 1846 repeal of the Corn Law. But the popular demonstrations of 1842 and 1848 had shown that immense popular pressure continued to be exerted on the old institutions because of the persistence of unacceptable living conditions. Reform was therefore vital, and was regarded as the only possible alternative to even more intense social conflict. (This motive was often openly admitted; for instance in the Report of the Health of Towns Commission of 1846, apropos of Bradford—where Titus Salt was Head Constable from 1845 and mayor from 1848—the lack of public open spaces is regretted because 'if the lower orders have not places where they can engage in sport and keep their minds engaged in matters of that kind, it is the very thing to drive them to Chartism'.[11])

The laws on subsidized housing were the result of this second wave of reform—promoted largely by Lord Shaftesbury—which was partly a continuation of the Whig reforms of the eighteen-thirties but which also embodied a new, markedly counter-revolutionary, bias.

In France the building experiments of the Second Empire were inspired by similar political preoccupations. Louis Napoleon, who

[10] Feargus O'Connor (1794–1855), leader of the Chartist movement, also organized a company for building workers' villages of very small houses and one of these, O'Connorville, was built at Herringsgate about 1845.
[11] Quoted in C. Stewart, *op. cit.*, p. 152.

had spent some time in England, knew of the English plans and experiments of the previous decade and had Henry Roberts' work —*Des Habitations des classes ouvrières*—translated in 1850.[12]

As President of the Republic, he granted 50,000 francs to subsidize the building of workers' dwellings in 1849 and directly financed the building of a residential complex for 500 people in the Rue Rochechouart, the Cité Napoléon.

During the years of the Empire he intensified these programmes, allocating 10 million francs in 1852—after the confiscation of the property of the Orléans—for workers' dwellings. In Paris he had the Cité Napoléon further enlarged, and built two other complexes: one at Batignolles, for 311 dwellings (1856–7) and one at Neuilly, for 120 dwellings (1867) which was given over to a co-operative society. For the Universal Exhibition of 1867 he gave his personal attention, as Prince Albert had done in 1851, to the construction of four model houses in the Avenue Rapp, offered a medal for the best working-class dwellings—won by the Société Coopérative Immobilière de Paris—and a series of very considerable money prizes for the best industrial complexes 'where social harmony and the well-being of the workers should prevail to the highest degree'.[13] A committee of Paris workers exhibited the 'maison des ouvriers à Paris' which they had built themselves, without either architects or contractors, after having been granted a subsidy of 20,000 francs by the Emperor.[14]

But private industry only very occasionally followed the Emperor's example and continued to encircle Paris with the wretched slums that housed the immigrants and people driven from the city centre by Haussmann's rebuilding. Felix Mornand wrote that in 1854 at Nonceau, which was just outside the city boundaries, a wine merchant built '40 plaster shacks each five foot by five, without windows—the light came in through the door, which had to be permanently open—without chimneys

[12] Cf. G. Lameyre, *Haussmann 'préfet de Paris'*, Paris, 1958, p. 163.
[13] *Op. cit.*, p. 163.
[14] *Op. cit.*, p. 162.

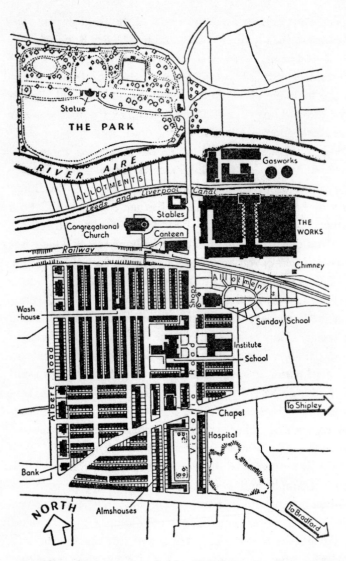

38 Plan of Saltaire, founded by T. Salt in 1851 (from C. Stewart, *A Prospect of Cities*).

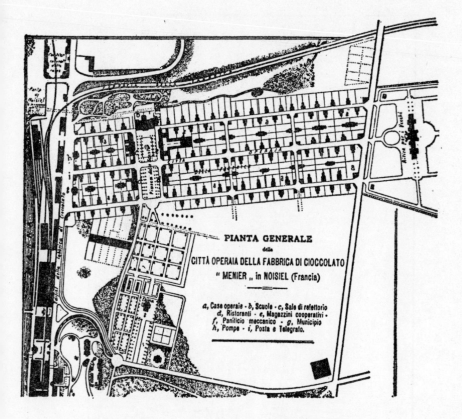

39 The 'Menier' Cité Ouvrière at Noisiel sur Marne (1864):
(a) workers' houses; (b) schools; (c) refectory; (d) restaurants;
(e) co-operative shops; (f) mechanised bakery; (g) town-hall; (h) fire
station; (o) post office and telegraph.

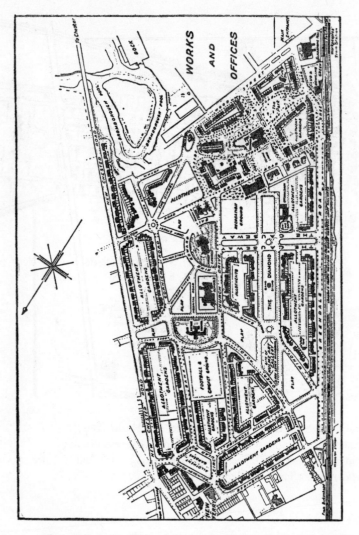

40   Plan of Port Sunlight, founded by W. H. Lever in 1887 (from
A. Whittick, *Modern Architecture*).

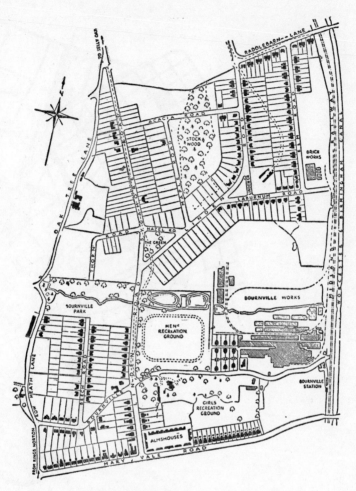

41   Plan of Bournville, founded by G. Cadbury in 1895 (from
P. L. Giordani, *L'Idea della citta-giardino*).

42 Florence, G. Poggi's development plan (1864–72) and clearance of the Mercato Vecchio, executed between 1885 and 1895. Parks are shown in cross hatching.

1   2 КМ

125

CASE D'OPERAJ.

43 Workers' dwellings at the Universal Exhibition in Paris, 1867.

and roofed with tar-lined paper. He rented each for 2 fr. or 2·50 a week, payable every Sunday, and thus earned himself 4,000 fr. a year'. Other shacks grew up around the city boundary, and 'it may be estimated that several thousand people, belonging to the most intelligent and most hard-working nation in the world, are housed in this manner'.[15]

Some more conscientious contractors tried to improve the standard of housing: for instance Puteaux, who built a special type of one-storey house for 2,150 fr., payable over fifteen years at a rate of 200 fr. a year, and Chauvelot, who sold small lots of suburban land 'for thrifty labourers, craftsmen and clerks, with the aim of attaching them to property, fount of law and order'.[16]

Various co-operative societies also worked along these lines, for instance the Société de Prévoyance which built the village La Sablière at Vincennes in 1855, and the Société de Co-opération

[15] F. Mornand, *La Vie à Paris*, Paris, 1855; G. Lameyre, *op. cit.*, p. 168.
[16] *Op. cit.*, p. 152.

44 French workers' dwellings built by the Anzim Company (from Godin).

appliqué au logement, which from 1866 onwards designed and built a special type of two-storey house costing 3,000 fr.

But the most important enterprise of the Second Empire was that of the Société Mulhousienne des Cités Ouvrières, founded in 1853 and financed both by private savings and by the State, which also paid for the relevant roads and open spaces. By 1867 over a thousand dwellings had been provided, one- or two-storey houses which were very small but which were sold or rented at very reasonable prices; normally, an advance of 250 or 300 fr. was required, and repayment was made at a rate of 18–20 fr. a month, over 15 years. A number of these houses were exhibited, very successfully, at the Paris exhibition in 1867.

In a report to the Société industrielle de Mulhouse, the aims of the enterprise were described as follows:

In the choice of the plan we are presenting to you today, we have been guided especially by the desire, which we share with you, to improve the conditions of workers both in the town and in the country, since the type of house is adapted to both. . . . The convenience and cleanliness of a man's lodging have a greater influence than might be thought on the morality and well-being of the family. If a man finds

45 Workers' houses provided by the Société Mulhousienne des Cités Ouvrières (from Godin).

his home wretched, filthy and disorderly, ill-smelling and unwholesome, he will not be at his ease there and will be happy to leave it for the tavern in the greater part of his free time. Thus he is a stranger in his own home and will soon develop into a spendthrift, to the great detriment of his own family, which is almost always reduced to destitution.

If we can offer these same men clean, attractive houses, if we can procure for each man a small garden, where he can find pleasant and useful employment, where caring for his own small harvest he can learn to value that feeling for ownership which Providence has instilled in us all, shall we not have solved one of the most important problems of social economy? Shall we not have contributed towards strengthening the sacred bonds of the family and rendered a true service to this class so worthy of concern, to our workers and to all society?[17]

Similar concerns were started in other countries, proportionately with the degree of industrialization. For example in Belgium, where the industrialist M. Degorge had started to build the village of Gran-Hornu as early as 1825; and in Germany, where the Krupp family completed the first group of workers' settlements

[17] Quoted in J. B. Godin, *Solutions sociales*. On Mulhouse see Engels, *The Housing Question, ed. cit.*, p. 58.

around Essen between 1863 and 1875 (Westend, Nordhof, Baum-hof, Kronenberg). In Italy, a model village was founded by the Poma, industrialists from Biella, in the Val d'Andorno.

The transformations that took place in the big cities from 1850 onwards—in Paris, Lyons, Brussels, Vienna, Barcelona, Florence —must be assessed in this political and ideological context.

The idea of a single comprehensive plan for a town implies the existence of an ideal model, distinct from and contrasting with reality; and during this period the idea of the city as a geometrical abstraction—as regular and uniform as the existing masses where shapeless and disorganized—came into its own once more.

Hygeia, planned by Benjamin W. Richardson (1828–96)[18] and Victoria, designed by John S. Buckingham (1786–1855)[19] were reminiscent of the ideal cities of the Renaissance not so much because they were their direct cultural descendants, as because they were produced by an analogous desire for order, in contra-distinction from the chaos that surrounded them. It was a similar love of system that inspired the first English regulations, and the by-law building that they produced.

Buckingham published his *Utopia* in 1849 and put forward his plan as a form of blueprint for mass production, to solve un-employment. Victoria, the first of these towns, occupied one square mile and contained seven concentric bands of buildings consisting of workers' dwellings, workshops, houses of superin-tendents and 'persons in charge of the several stores for the distribution and supply of all the articles required for the use of

18 Cf. C. Stewart, *op. cit.*, p. 169.
19 J. S. Buckingham, *National Evils and Practical Remedies*; cf. Stewart, *op. cit.*, pp. 168–72. Buckingham sums up Victoria's aims as follows: 'The objects chiefly kept in view have been to unite the greatest degree of order, symmetry, space and healthfulness, in the largest supply of air and light, and in the most perfect system of drainage, with the comfort and convenience of all classes . . . ready accessibility to all parts of the town under continuous shelter from sun and rain when necessary, with the disposition of the public buildings in such localities as to make them easy of approach from all quarters, and surrounded with space for numerous avenues of entrance and exit. And in addition to all these a large admixture of grass lawn, garden ground and flowers, and an abundant supply of water—the whole to be united with an elegance and economy as may be found practical.' (Quoted in T. Sharp, *English Panorama*, London, 1950, pp. 73–4.)

46 Workers' houses at Grand-Hornu, Belgium (from Godin).

the town', shops, houses of professional people, public pro-
menades and the houses of the wealthy. In the centre were the
public buildings, the houses of the 'members of the government
and the wealthiest capitalists', and a large square with a tower
300 feet high bearing a beacon to illuminate the whole city.

Buckingham's plan was in some ways reminiscent of that of
Owen. It was put forward as a remedy for unemployment, it was
a blueprint from which many versions could be made, it was in
the form of a square and contained all the most modern sanitary
arrangements. Both Buckingham and Richardson insist on the
importance of hygiene: fresh air, light, water, even washable
clothes and floors polished with bees wax 'which generates health-
giving ozone'.[20] Industry and the more insalubrious public services take place at a prudent distance from the town centre.

The fundamental change to be noted was that the geometrical
and technical aspects of town-planning were now accepted, while
political and economic considerations had been discarded. It was
in this attenuated form that the contribution of the socialist

[20] C. Stewart, *op. cit.*, p. 168.

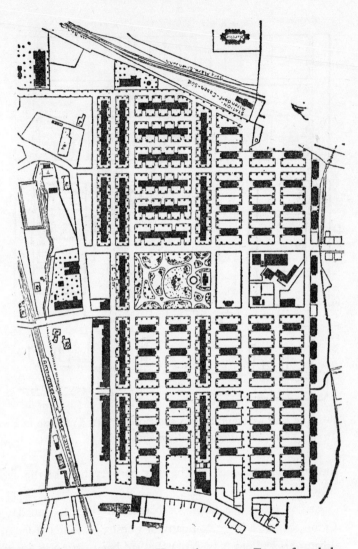

47 Plan of workers' settlement at Kronenberg, near Essen, founded by the Krupps in 1873 (from B. Zevi, *Storia dell' Archittura Moderna*).

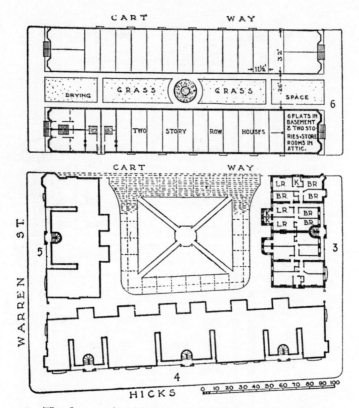

48 The first workers' houses sponsored by A. T. White in Brooklyn (from C. Gray, *Housing and Citizenship*).

theorists was adopted by the new conservatism of the eighteen-fifties.[21]

Arsène Houssaye wrote of Napoleon III that one day at St. Cloud, before a large company of guests, he told a story of how, during his exile in New York, he had been sitting in a restaurant next to some down-and-out who 'unrolled a great scroll of paper

[21] It would be interesting to study the use made of these concepts in English colonial town-planning, particularly during the second half of the nineteenth century. A starting point is provided by E. G. Wakefield's book *Art of Colonization* (London, 1849) mentioned by Howard in Ch. X of *Tomorrow*. There is also a book by R. Pemberton, *The Happy Colony* (London, 1854), where a Utopia similar to that of Buckingham is described; see S. Lang's article 'The Ideal City' in *Architectural Review*, August 1952.

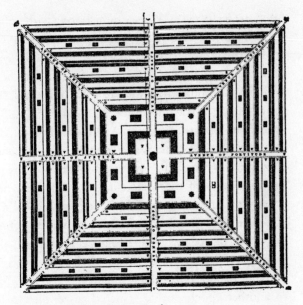

49   Plan of Victoria (J. S. Buckingham, 1849).

on which he had designed a city for twenty thousand inhabitants, with churches, fountains, squares, monuments and, of course, a stock exchange . . . a real city of the future, such as we shall have here in France . . . no longer will one house be built at a time, he said, but the whole will be begun on the same day and all shall be finished at the same time.

'What I am telling you,' went on Napoleon, 'may sound like a fairy tale, but this man was being quite serious; he had already begun negotiations for the sites and buildings; he had taken his contracts to bankers, who had smelt a fortune in the business for them just as this fellow did for himself . . . That very day I swore that, on my return to Paris—for I never doubted that I would return—I would build the capital of capitals, as indeed I have begun to do, with God's help.'[22]

The perfect executor of such a scheme, a man who never con-

[22] A. Houssaye, *Les Confessions: souvenirs d'un demi-siècle, 1830–80*, Paris, 1885; quoted in G. Lameyre, *op. cit.*, p. 92.

fused the technical and the administrative with politics, was Baron Haussmann, Prefect of the Seine from 1853 to 1869.

Haussmann's personal views were strictly conservative. In 1850, on leaving the Prefecture of the Var, he described his political position as follows. He wished, he said, 'to unite, under the standard of law and order, by means of a just conciliation of decent and impartial opinions, all men whole-heartedly dedicated to the good of the country and to those primary concerns on which all society is founded'.[23] Soon afterwards, in his first circular to the employees of the prefecture of the Yonne, he wrote: 'Two years ago, amid the confusion engendered by a revolution as complete as it was unexpected, at a moment when all the basic principles of society were being debated anew, this department turned, almost unanimously, to the heir of a name which stirred undying memories of glory, but which also drew men's thoughts to another epoch during which France, after a long period of revolutionary agitation and anarchy, saw the rule of law, the respect of authority and the veneration of all that is sacred blossom forth once more, in the shadow of a popular power, and saw security, confidence and public prosperity come forth again as if by enchantment,[24] and, in 1851, when he was appointed Prefect of the Gironde, he added, with significant emphasis: 'Men of disorder need expect no indulgence from me.'[25]

It was therefore natural that Haussmann should give un-qualified support to the future Napoleon III and should remain faithful to him until the fall of the Empire. But, precisely because he did have the Emperor's support, Haussmann was always able to avoid having to justify his actions politically and could present them as technical and administrative measures deriving from objective necessities. This appeal to objectivity was sometimes a tactical expedient, but it did often reveal a genuine conviction that planning measures were indeed reducible to mere technical and administrative calculation. Haussmann expressed this con-

[23] *Op. cit.*, p. 19.
[24] *Op. cit.*, p. 20.
[25] *Op. cit.*, p. 24.

viction when he said that 'in France, a good act well explained is always an act sanctioned',[26] thus applying the Cartesian theory of necessary assent to clear and well-formulated ideas to the sphere of administration.

Haussmann set the pattern for the town-planner as a specialist worker who declines all responsibility for initial choice, and therefore in practice for the town-planner who is at the service of the new ruling class.

Yet the modern and positive aspects of his work are to be found precisely in the independence he allows himself, as a pure administrator, *vis-à-vis* other State departments.

Haussmann's considerable achievements of bringing all public works under one control, of making investment in them no longer a risk, since repayment of the loans could now be guaranteed by the future productivity of these works, and of reorganizing the administrative districts at the same time as their redevelopment, were only realized after a long and difficult struggle against other sectors of the administration and with his own political superiors. The main conflict arose over the interpretation of the law of 13 April on the redevelopment of slum property, mentioned in the previous chapter.

Article 13 of the law, as has been said, legalized the acquisition of all the property within the area in which there was work to be done.

Haussmann tried to interpret the law in such a way that the various building sites acquired and improved by the administration, should remain public property and be sold at their new market value. But the Council of State decided, on 27 September 1858, that the Commune should retain only the roads, while the surrounding areas should be restored to their original owners.

The new decision, deliberated *motu proprio* by this great assembly, not only imperilled the precious authority already granted to the 'Cité', to acquire sites outside the routes of the roads that are to be

[26] Haussmann's speech to the Conseil communal de Paris, 14 Nov. 1859; *op. cit.*, p. 118.

opened up and considered necessary for the construction of adequate and sanitary houses, but it also gave the owners of the relevant buildings the right to retain all the land not destined for public use, after causing the 'Cité' to pay for the value of the buildings originally standing on the land, as well as for the compensation of the former inhabitants. In this way the original landlord was presented, quite gratuitously, with the benefit of the increase in the value of the land, now made available, thanks to the Municipality, for a more profitable use, fronting on to a fine wide road; while the Municipality was deprived of the opportunity of recovering some part of the considerable expenses incurred as a result of this undertaking, by selling the sites at an advantageous price.[27]

Here Haussmann had sensed one of the basic problems of modern planning (he was opposed, let us remember, by the Liberal opposition who were defending, in the words of Jules Ferry, 'a right consistently recognized by our laws'[28]) and in this case refused to accept the political logic of the régime which he personally supported so whole-heartedly.

Nevertheless, his opposition was fruitless because it set out to defend the rights of an abstract administrative entity ('the city') against the concrete rights of the citizens. This is the contradiction at the heart of Haussmann's ideas, and one which was to remain unresolved in the history of town-planning for some time to come.

The political left, for its own part, failed to sense this contradiction and consequently failed to draw a distinction, in concrete terms, between the potential revolutionary significance of many

[27] G. E. Haussmann, *Mémoires,* Paris, 1890, vol. II, pp. 310–11.
[28] J. Ferry, *Comptes fantastiques d'Haussmann,* Paris, 1868, p. 23.

50 OPPOSITE Plan of Haussmann's *grands travaux* in Paris. The heavy black lines show new roads opened in old quarters, the lighter ones roads built in the suburbs, in districts previously not built up. New districts are shown in cross-hatching, public parks in hatching. The city's new administrative boundary coincides with Thiers' fortifications, but the built-up area extended well beyond them, along the main roads out of the city.

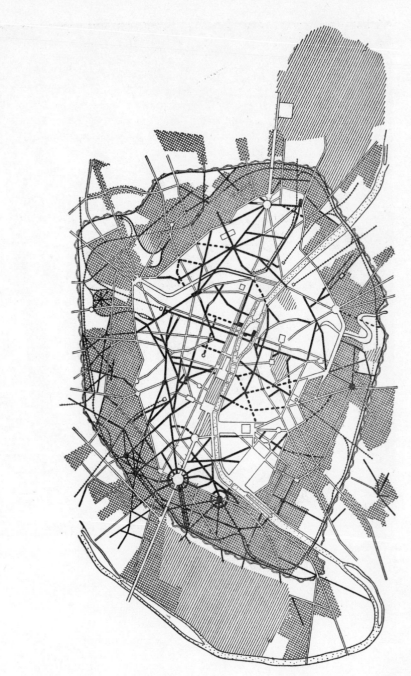

137

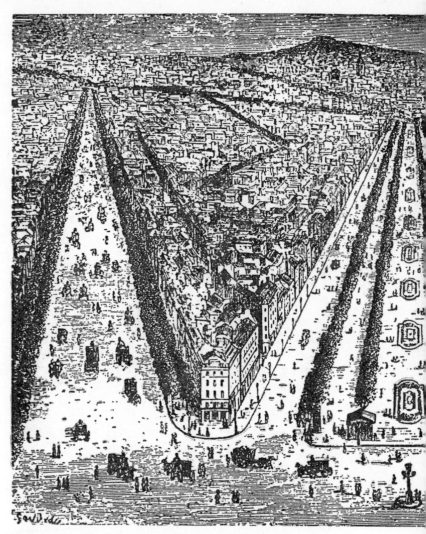

51   Paris, view of the city along the Boulevard Richard Lenoir
(from S. Giedion, *Space, Time and Architecture*).

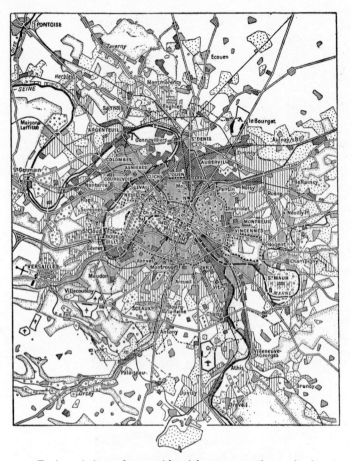

52   Paris as it is to-day; residential zones are shown by hatching or
dots, industrial zones by cross-hatching (from P. George, *Les Villes*).

53 OPPOSITE   The growth of London from 1748 to 1939; the two
circles have diameters of ten and twenty miles (from Stephenson and
Pool, *A Plan for Town and Country*).

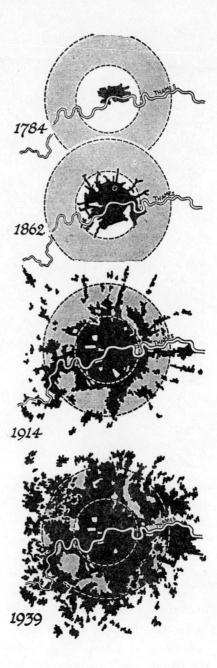

1784

1862

1914

1939

54 The main public works round the city of London (shown in hatching) in the second half of the nineteenth century; new roads are shown in heavy black, railways in the traditional manner.

pieces of town-planning and the conservative bias with which most of them were certainly implemented.

Engels wrote a typical series of articles on the housing problem in 1872, in answer to writings of Mülberger. They were published in 1872 in the Leipzig *Volkstaat* and were collected in a single volume under the title *Wohnungsfrage*. Mülberger had expounded the theories of Proudhon and Sax, described the experimental

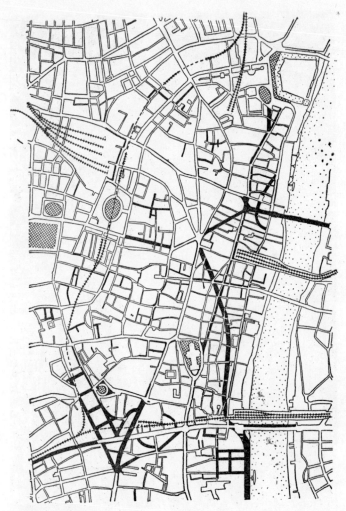

55 The new roads opened in the City in Victorian times.

cités ouvrières in France and the English villages and building societies as models for dawning German industrialism. In reply Engels demonstrated that the ownership of a house, generally provided by employer or the State and purchased with the worker's own means, still did not free him from capitalist exploitation, indeed it enabled the capitalist to lower wages in accordance

56 A view of part of London in 1851, published by Banks and Co.;
houses and factories are inextricably mingled on both sides of the
river.

with the amount of unpaid rent and lessened the workers' mobility, i.e. his chances to withdraw from the conditions laid down by his employer. Furthermore, philanthropic attempts to improve the quality of housing did not abolish, but merely displaced the slums and poor quarters necessarily connected with the methods of capitalist production, to other districts.

Engels' criticism was based mainly on the situation in Germany at this time. German industry was in its infancy and could compete with France and England only by keeping production costs at a minimum and this was made possible chiefly by settling workers in the country or in suburban settlements, as owners of houses with plots of land, from which they could earn an income which alone would have been inadequate for survival but which was sufficient when taken together with the low wages offered by industry.

Competition permits the capitalist to deduct from the price of labour that which the family earns from its own little garden or field; the workers are compelled to accept any piece wages offered to them, because otherwise they would get nothing at all, and they could not live from the products of their small scale agriculture alone and because, on the other hand, it is just this agriculture and landownership which chains them to the spot and prevents them from looking around for other enployment. This is the basis which upholds Germany's capacity to compete on the world market in a whole series of small articles. The whole capital profit is derived from a deduction from normal wages and the whole surplus value can be presented to the purchaser.[29]

This reasoning was sufficient for Engels to discount all previous building experiments and to refuse even to discuss them. He presented the contradiction between the humanitarian aim—that of improving the workers' living conditions—and the capitalist tendency to keep these conditions low, in order to reduce the cost of labour, simply as a piece of deception to be exposed, while in fact it had been a constant feature of earlier experiments and one which had touched off a complex chain of actions and reactions.

[29] F. Engels, *op. cit.*, p. 13.

Engels did not even attempt to formulate any alternative programme to replace the dreams and calculations of the reforming *bourgeoisie*. To take an example, the thesis of the mobility of labour, vital for the conservation of the worker's bargaining power, would seem to imply living patterns quite different from the one-family houses of suburban settlements, something along the lines of the multi-storey blocks with standard accommodation and communal services suggested by modern town-planners between the wars; but Engels preferred to regard the future organization of the towns as a mere consequence of the general economic revolution towards which the working-class movement must move, and to regard the question of housing as an implicit and inseparable part of the general problems of society.

Thus Marxist critique, though it formulated several basic principles for the interpretation of the experiments that were actually taking place, said nothing about their application in the specific field of planned building and thus cut itself off from the development of town-planning for many years.

Subsequent progress was made not deductively, by applying the findings of political theory to the field of town-planning; but inductively, from repeated experience of individual difficulties and conflicts, and this inspired some of the most dedicated thinkers on the subject to trace back the chain of cause and effect to its source, extending their field of enquiry until they discovered the lost link between the technical and the political.

The development of William Morris, for instance, followed this course. Originally a member of a circle not unlike the Young England group, and starting from an awareness of the ugliness of the industrial landscape, he gradually brought to light the political and economic factors which were preventing any possible remedy, and arrived independently at Socialism to the extent, in fact, of becoming active in the English workers' movement. The personal case of William Morris reflects the development of most of European thought and literature on the subject of town-planning.

Just as the technical proposals of the Utopians were to be easily separated from social innovations and utilized by paternalistic reformists precisely to conserve the social balance threatened by the Revolution, so the various enterprises fostered by conservative forces, once realized, were able to develop in a sense completely contrary to that of their original conception and, subsequently, be transformed into weapons to overturn the systems they had been supposed to consolidate.

Thus the Napoleonic *cités ouvrières*, the model English villages and Krupp settlements were the first links in a chain of experiments which were to lead to Garnier's *cités industrielles*, the districts designed by Berlage, the *Siedlungen* of Frankfort and Vienna. At this point the facts call for a new confrontation of the respective programmes of town-planning and politics, to try and bridge the gulf that opened between them a hundred years ago. This is the task that faces us today.

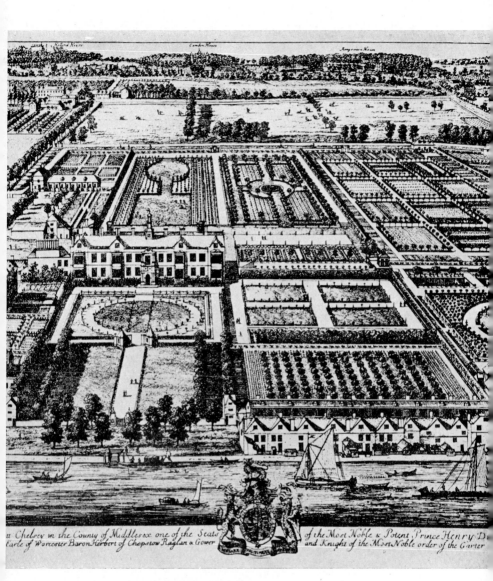

Within the engraving:

at Chelsey in the County of Middlesex one of the Seats
Earle of Worcester Baron Herbert of Chepstow Raglan & Gower

of the Most Noble & Potent Prince Henry D
and Knight of the Most Noble order of the Garter

1   A stretch of Baroque landscape—the suburban residence of the Earl of Worcester in Chelsea, Middlesex—where buildings and formally laid-out gardens are consciously placed within a natural setting. The relationship between formal and natural is regarded as permanent; the architecture is the focal point, creating the vital harmony

2 and 3   Town and country are invaded by all the concomitants
of the new industrial economy, which is in rapid and continual flux;
cities are surrounded, the margins of the natural countryside are
pushed back. The face of the country is constantly changing; its
growth is complex and irregular because there exist no instruments
to control its particular mechanism of development

4 and 5 In contrast with the sprawling chaos of the new suburbs
was the absolute regularity of the monumental early nineteenth-
century architectural complexes (the Nash terraces around Regent's
Park in London and the façades by Percier and Fontaine along the
Rue de Rivoli in Paris). But architectural regularity was only an
expedient to give uniformity to a branch of building activity which,
even here, escaped administrative control. Behind the uniform
façades, individual contractors continued to work when and how
they pleased, unconcerned with any comprehensive plan

6   Count Duriveau announcing the setting up of the Phalanstère to his employees (illustration in *Les miserès des enfants trouvés* by Eugène Sue, in the *Biblioteca romantica illustrata*)

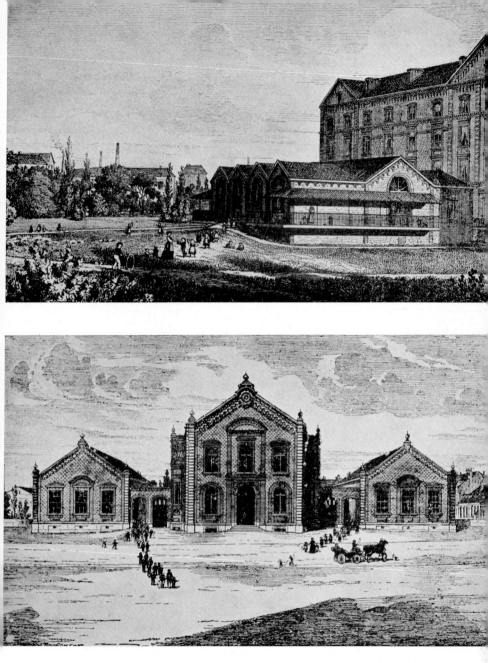

7 and 8 Two views of Jean Baptiste Godin's Familistère at Guise:
the nursery, adjoining the main body of the *palais social*, and the
school buildings and theatre (from J. B. Godin, *Solutions Sociales*)

9 The interior of the nursery adjoining the Familistère (J. B. Godin, *Solutions Sociales*)

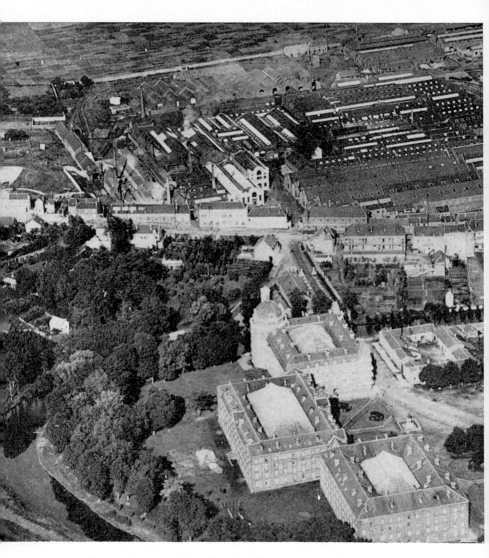

10   Aerial view of Godin's Familistère as it is today; the relation
between the residential blocks, surrounded by trees, and the factory,
has been retained despite alterations and developments (from
R. Auzelle, *Encyclopédie de l'urbanisme*)

11 The other nineteenth-century proposal to bring the industrial
landscape back to human scale: the garden city (view of
Letchworth); but the delicate balance between space for private
accommodation and productive activities, propounded by Howard,
was unable to withstand the uneven pull exerted by these factors,
and Howard's proposal became a mere formal model for the
planning of town suburbs

12 Unaffected by proposals and experiments, the city outskirts of
the late nineteenth-century continued to grow, regulated only by
the unthinking application of building restrictions. Roads and
houses stretched away endlessly, as far as it was economically
convenient to build them

13   The city street, conceived and designed during the second half
of the nineteenth century according to the canons of Baroque
regularity, was in fact completely transformed by the traffic and
permanent trivia which it was destined to accommodate—crowds,
vehicles, shop signs, general clutter; these assumed pride of place,
so that the original basic architecture seemed to recede into the
background (photograph of Rue Richelieu, Paris, 1904)

14 and 15   Two of Haussmann's streets, Ave. Wagram and Ave.
Foch, seen from the top of the Arc de Triomphe. The first, a
typical street in the new and smart district of the Étoile, was
designed to offer building speculators a reasonable opportunity to
make the most of the adjacent sites; behind the façades facing on to

the avenue, space had to be used as economically as possible, with
minimum distance between the houses. The second, conceived as the
main entrance to the Bois de Boulogne, is a great avenue bordered
by trees, one of the finest achievements of Haussmann's authoritarian
planning

16 The Île de la Cité in Paris, after Haussmann's radical
transformation. The only small group of old buildings surviving,
a reminder of the humble origins of the old city centre, are those
along the north flank of Notre Dame; isolated monuments have
been restored—the cathedral, the Palais de Justice—but they are
completely surrounded by the great new buildings and the spacious
streets